An Alliance of Spirit:
Museum and School Partnerships

An Alliance of Spirit:
Museum and School Partnerships

Edited by Kim Fortney and Beverly Sheppard

The AAM Press
American Association of Museums
Washington, DC

An Alliance of Spirit: Museum and School Partnerships

Edited by Kim Fortney and Beverly Sheppard

©2010 The AAM Press, American Association of Museums, 1575 Eye St. NW, Suite 400, Washington, DC 20005.

The opinions expressed by the authors in this book are their own and are not to be taken as representing the views of any institution or organization, including the American Association of Museums.

Library of Congress Cataloging-in-Publication Data

An alliance of spirit : museum and school partnerships / edited by Kim
Fortney and Beverly Sheppard.
   p. cm.
Includes bibliographical references.
ISBN 978-1-933253-16-9 (alk. paper)
1. Museums and schools--United States. 2. Museums--Educational
aspects--United States. I. Kim, Fortney. II. Sheppard, Beverly, 1941-
LB1047.A45 2010
371.3'84--dc22
                2010015004
ISBN 978-1-933253-16-9

Cover photos: Top photo ©Bruce Guthrie. All others: Courtesy Smithsonian American Art Museum. Special thanks to the Public Affairs staff at the Smithsonian American Art Museum.

The Smithsonian American Art Museum is a leader in providing resources to schools and the public through its national education programs. Among its many educational initiatives, students use art as a primary resource and experience hands-on activities, interactive games, student podcasts and directed writing exercises. Support from the William Randolph Hearst Endowment for America's Artistic Heritage and the David and Lucille Packard Foundation makes possible two partnerships with Washington, D.C. public schools, *Creating American Stories* and transportation to the museum for every sixth-grade student for two years. The museum offers *Artful Connections*, real-time video conference tours worldwide. Educators as individuals, teams or departments learn to use art with technology as a cross-disciplinary tool through The Clarice Smith National Teacher Institutes, workshops and in-service programs. Gallaudet University deaf students and faculty are gallery guides to deaf and hearing visitors in *Art Signs*, also available online.

Designed by Polly Franchini
Printed by Gray Graphics

Contents

Acknowledgments

A PROJECT of this magnitude is the work of many hands and minds. In addition to our exceedingly patient family members, the editors and authors are deeply grateful to the following individuals and institutions for their creativity, expertise, editing skills and support:

Joe Alfano, Science Curriculum Specialist, Minneapolis Public Schools; The AAM Press of the American Association of Museums; Bakken Museum educators and Teachers in Residence, past and present; Sibyl Barnum, Arts Impact Director/ Director Arts Education, Puget Sound Educational Service District, Renton, Washington; Barbara Bassett, Philadelphia Museum of Art; Jennifer Berg, Manhattan High School, Manhattan, Kansas; Lauren Berkley; Rachel Bernstein, Senior Education Coordinator, Professional Development for Teachers, Los Angeles County Museum of Art; Tanya Brown-Merriman, former teacher (Art Education) and museum educator; John Buchinger, Associate Director of Education, New York State Historical Association; Steve Bullick, Mt. Lebanon School District, Mt. Lebanon, Pennsylvania; Lonnie G. Bunch, III, Founding Director, National Museum of African American History and Culture; Mary Case, Founding Director, Qm2; Carolyn Chernoff, Institute of Contemporary Art, University of Pennsylvania; Ryjil Christianson, Pratt Museum; Stephanie J. Coakley, Tucson Museum of Art and Historic Block; Laura Creed, The Barnes Foundation; Andrea Del Valle, Brooklyn Historical Society; Sharon Dietz, Enrichment Facilitator, J. P. McCaskey High School, School District of Lancaster, Lancaster, Pennsylvania; Rene Fehr, Westmoreland Elementary School, Manhattan, Kansas; Margaret Fitzgerald, Middle School 577, Brooklyn, New York; Ben Garcia, Skirball Cultural Center; Cathy Gorn, Executive Director, National History Day; Bay Hallowell, Philadelphia Museum of Art; Barbara Henry, Oakland Museum of California; Sarah Holloran, Pennsylvania Academy of the Fine Arts; Sandra Jenkins, Science Teacher, Stuart-Hobson Middle School, Washington, D.C.; Rita Johnson, Principal, Nannie Helen Burroughs Elementary School, Washington, D.C.; Maribel Jusino-Iturralde, The New Jersey Historical Society; Lynda Kennedy, Woodside, New York; Amanda Kodeck, Manager, School Programs, Walters Art Museum; Christine Kola, Middle School 45, Brooklyn, New York; Rebecca Krucoff, Urban Memory Project; Kari Kufahl, Westmoreland Elementary School; Westmoreland, Kansas; Adrienne Lee, Natural History Museum of Los Angeles County; Larry Liotta, Amanda Arnold Elementary School, Manhattan, Kansas; Ted Lind, Deputy Director for Education, The Newark Museum; Lynne Long, EdD, former museum school principal and professional development specialist, Washington, D.C.; The Mid-Atlantic Association of Museums; Tracey Mina, Early Childhood Educator; Dianne Moore-Williams, Mentor Teacher; Beth Nietzel, Susan B. Anthony Middle School, Manhattan, Kansas; Suzanne Otto, Woodrow Wilson Elementary School, Manhattan, Kansas; The Pennsylvania Federation of Museums and Historical Organizations; Johanna Plummer, Institute of Contemporary Art, University of Pennsylvania; Qm2 Directors Roundtable members; Judy Ringold, Pennsylvania Academy of the Fine Arts; Christina Roberts, The Fabric Workshop and Museum; Nancy Rosner, The Barnes Foundation; Sophie Sanders, The Fabric Workshop and Museum; Erika Sanger, Director of Education, Albany Institute of History & Art; Patricia Sigala, Museum of International Folk Art; Marcos A. Stafne, Head of Education & Visitor Experience, Rubin Museum of Art; Carol B. Stapp, Director, Museum Education Program, The George Washington University; Tim Taglauer, Education Specialist, Shenandoah National Park; Sarah Thayer, Lehigh County Historical Society; April Tonin, The Nightingale-Bamford School, New York; Kathy F. Wagner, Independent Consultant; Kris Wetterlund, Sandbox Studios; Jennifer Willson, Manager of School, Educator, and Interpretive Technology programs, Seattle Art Museum; Myron Yoder, Allentown School District, Allentown, Pennsylvania; Jeffrey Zeiders, Social Studies Advisor, Pennsylvania Department of Education; Monica Zimmerman, Pennsylvania Academy of the Fine Arts.

Foreword

✺ ✺ ✺

AS MUSEUM EDUCATORS, schools are a natural target audience for us. We spend tremendous time, resources, and energy trying to reach and engage students and teachers. Years ago, we developed and implemented an after-school program for young girls called Girls At the Museum Exploring Science (GAMES) at the University of Colorado Museum of Natural History. Although the program was thoroughly conceived, planned, and executed, it struggled to find its footing at first. With the development of a strong partnership between the museum and the local school district, the GAMES program gained significant sustaining support and resources from the University and outside funding agencies, as well as winning a regional award for excellence in museum education.

With the publication of *An Alliance of Spirit: Museum and School Partnerships,* brought up to date with a selection of new authors and chapters, we have a valuable new resource to use to engage this key audience. The first edition, published in 1993, contains information and guidelines for educators that are timeless and still relevant today, yet some of the content seems dated. Where are we now in relation to partnerships between museums and schools? What are the attributes of a successful relationship and how do you establish and sustain such a relationship? This updated volume contains a mixture of "toolbox" information and case studies, making it immensely useful to museum educators and teachers alike, whether graduate students, emerging professionals, or seasoned educators. This revised edition melds a growing body of theoretical work and the expertise of practitioners into a practical guide.

The American Association of Museums' Education Committee (EdCom) advances the purpose of museums as places of lifelong learning, serves as an advocate for diverse audiences and educators, and promotes professional standards and excellence in the practice of museum education. The work of the Committee is to provide service to its membership and to the field, in part through professional development opportunities and resources. Over the past year, a Task Force of the EdCom Board has consulted with the editors and reviewed drafts of the chapters of this edition. The Committee is very pleased to endorse this new edition for our members and for the field. We are confident that *An Alliance of Spirit: Museum and School Partnerships* will offer the field an important and needed update on the topic, and will provide both a strong theoretical framework and hands-on practical advice.

Jim S. H. Hakala
Chair, American Association of Museums' Education Committee

Introduction

✳ ✳ ✳

IN THE CLASSIC NOVEL *The Catcher in the Rye*, the lead character Holden Caulfield recalls his classroom visits to the museum of natural history. He describes a flood of sensory impressions: standing in line holding a classmate's sweaty hand, the sound of a dropped marble clattering across the floor, the dark cavernous halls, the brightly-lit glass cases filled with intricate dioramas.

"The best thing in the museum," he tells us, "was that everything always stayed right where it was. Nobody'd move. You could go there a hundred thousand times, and the Eskimo would still be just finished catching those two fish, the birds would still be on their way south, the deer would still be drinking out of that water hole, with their pretty antlers and their pretty skinny legs, and that squaw with the naked bosom would still be weaving that same blanket. Nobody'd be different. The only thing that would be different would be you."[1]

One can only wonder how Holden would describe a field trip experience today. Would he still be quietly in line, following a docent through the halls? Would he be passively looking into an exhibit case? Would he still find rows of silent dioramas frozen in time? Or would Holden's museum visit today invite his participation in hands-on learning? Would it empower him to make his own discoveries and talk about them with his classmates and teachers? Would he combine his encounters with real things with the tools of technology, building layers of meaning and understanding? What changes would be most striking in today's field trip experience? What experiences would feel familiar and bound to the past? What is the magic of the museum and school partnership that has enabled it to endure for so long, remaining a staple for both museums and schools?

Museums and schools have a long history of working together. *Museums for a New Century*, a 1989 publication of the American Association of Museums, refers to this history as "perhaps the most longstanding and successful example of the interest and ability of museums to join forces with other institutions in working toward common goals."[2] The museum and school partnership has been written about for many decades by many successful practitioners committed to sharing their learning. This enduring collaboration represents one of the very few intersections that exist between formal and informal education, allowing the strengths of both to combine into a learning experience unlike any other.

When *Building Museum and School Partnerships* was first published in 1993, it sought to express the essence of late 20th-century thinking and practice, combining theory with practical application. Today, in a new century, museum and school educators are updating their work, refreshing their partnerships to reflect ever-changing environments.

Technology has brought powerful new opportunities to our work: expanding communication, enriching content sharing, offering greater accessibility to experts and programs, field trip extensions, widened partnerships, international connections and learning formats for all. Reform movements have led to the adoption of learning standards in many disciplines, new requirements in accountability, and stricter controls over teaching time. Population diversity has redefined communities across the country, enriching classrooms with greater ethnicity, racial diversity, new customs, traditions and languages, and the challenge to integrate, not isolate our newcomers.

Rethinking the potential of true partnerships between museums and schools is essential. It has been a great pleasure and inspiration to work with Kim Fortney on this process. As an engaged museum educator, committed to providing the highest quality of learning experiences, Kim has drawn from her breadth of experience and expertise to assemble a timely publication and bring together outstanding authors.

The chapters ahead explore many topics, all tied to what it means to think together, plan together, and execute together—all for the enrichment of the students we serve. Editors Beverly Sheppard and Kim Fortney, along with educator Mark D. Osterman, retain a focus on the basics, emphasizing the collaborative nature of museums and schools developing strong programs. Maria Marable-Bunch draws on her extensive conversations with teachers to deepen our understanding of their perspectives and needs. Kathrine Walker Schlageck examines the impact of No Child Left Behind and an increasing emphasis on learning standards in today's classroom. She also includes an overview of how technology is expanding the reach and practice of both classroom and museum programming,

Authors Beth Twiss Houting, Mary Jane Taylor and Susy Watts provide an important analysis of learning theories that support educational programs in the museum setting. The use and understanding of tested theory as a basis of museum teaching is an indicator of the increasing professionalism of the museum-based educational experience. This professionalism is further emphasized in Chapter 7 where three authors, Kim Fortney, Susy Watts and James Boyer, describe the growing significance and quality of professional development programs for teachers, clearly an expanding and influential area for partnerships. Assuring relevance and adding evaluation methodologies likewise add to the quality of museum programs as presented by Julia Washburn and Beth Murphy. And three authors, Betsy Bowers, Jennifer Michaelree Squire, and Mary Jane Taylor, remind us of the challenge of funding our partnership programs in difficult times. They offer an analysis of the issue, provide funding strategies, and re-emphasize the importance of evaluation data as a key to ongoing support.

Several chapters present examples of how the museum and school collaboration continues to respond to community changes. Claudia Ocello illustrates the creativity within museum programming that expands beyond specific disciplines to meet emerging needs and teaching opportunities. The museum-school partnership as a catalyst to reach even deeper into the community is explored by Janet Rassweiler and Julie I. Johnson. Their work demonstrates how the art of partnership can support deep impact on community needs of all kinds. A powerful new development in the arena of museum and school partnerships is described by Sonnet Takahisa and Ron Chaluisan, the founders of the The New York City Museum School, a school that places museum learning at the core of the curriculum. In a follow-up piece, Keni Sturgeon provides a listing of other museum schools, developed through a variety of structures and relationships.

The reader will find many tools for supporting the partnership work of their own institutions. Case studies, tips and guidelines, and additional resources appear throughout the book. Ann Fortescue, Marla Shoemaker, James Stein, Jean Woodley, Laura Dickstein Thompson, and additional contributors Amy Goicoechea, Ellen Provenzano, Ellen Strojan, and Courtney Waring have all added ideas, examples, and insights from their teaching experiences. The authors thank the many museum professionals they interviewed during the development of the book. Those acknowledgments follow this introduction.

The editors appreciate the support of all who have made this book so thorough and rich. We hope it will be well used to support and inspire that most productive collaboration—the museum and school partnership.

Beverly Sheppard, Co-Editor

NOTES

1. J.D. Salinger, *The Catcher in the Rye* (New York: Grosset and Dunlap, 1951).

2. Ellen Cochran Hicks, *Museums for a New Century* (Washington, D.C: American Association of Museums, 1984), 66.

Museums and Schools Working Together

Mark D. Osterman and Beverly Sheppard

Chapter One establishes the fundamental requirements at the heart of strong and enduring museum and school partnerships, stressing the need for clear expectations, mutual respect, and a meaningful level of shared values. The necessity for deep collaboration, carefully and thoughtfully developed, is at the core of each succeeding chapter.

❋ ❋ ❋

Museums and schools are natural partners and have, for years, demonstrated the essence of meaningful collaboration. When museums and schools partner, students learn through multiple formats—reading and writing, looking and examining. They use the power of observation to fuel new questions and apply thinking skills to the act of discovery. They learn in a social setting in the museum and in a more solitary process in their classroom studies. These are complementary experiences, providing multiple ways for students to learn. Museums provide the magic of encounter, complementing the more abstract ideas discussed in the classroom. Teachers in both are committed to the same educational goals, and the results of their working together can lead to deep levels of student understanding. No wonder these partnerships have lasted so long!

In this opening chapter the authors examine the basic questions at the heart of the museum and school partnership, examining field trip experiences and other learning opportunities. The chapter investigates several key questions: What do museums and schools need to understand about one another to build sustainable and cogent partnerships? What preparation and follow-up should each expect of the other? What unique gifts do they bring to one another? What logistical needs must be met? These are the questions that opened *Building Museum and School Partnerships*,[1] the forerunner of this book. On the surface, they are simple and straightforward, but answering them *together* is the key to success.

The class field trip offers a logical beginning for this inquiry. It is what most schools and museums think of as the staple of their long partnership. In fact, there are many reasons to consider it one of the common experiences of childhood and one that has long-lasting impact. In "Recalling the Museum Experience," an article written for the *Journal of Museum Education*, authors John H. Falk and Lynn D. Dierking cite a number of studies that relate to museum memories.[2] One in particular interviewed 128 individuals, both students and adults, about their recollections of school field trips. Overall, 96% could recall their experiences, and all but two were able to cite specific memories with great clarity and detail. Their memories were remarkably vivid, including details of content, setting, and social interaction. Such findings make it very clear that the field trip, especially one developed through partnership, should be regarded as a powerful teaching tool.

Successful collaboration is never guaranteed. Even the highest-minded intentions can end in mediocre or even failed results, so working within the guiding tenets of good partnerships is essential. Schools and museums are very different institutions in so many ways. Yet each has the common mission of serving the learner and offering the richest possible learning experience for all of the students engaged. The school and museum partnership brings formal and informal together in mutual support. The best results will occur when the rules of partnership are actively applied, beginning with an agreed upon set of expectations and a commitment to knowing each other as thoroughly as possible.

In the first edition of this book 17 years ago, the opening chapters asked two complementary questions: "What do museums want from schools?" and, "What do schools want from museums?" Answers stressed good communication, collaborative planning, and mutual empathy for what it takes on both sides to plan and execute a successful visit. Museums want students to arrive excited and curious, prepared to learn through the pre-visit materials they have carefully written and sent well in advance. They want teachers and chaperones to have worked out the logistics of the visit, following their instructions for dividing up the students into pre-arranged small groups, with the school-provided adults taking responsibility for behavior and discipline. Their hope is to step into a lesson already set in motion and relate the richness of the museum exhibitions to eager learners.

Teachers may have different perspectives. They have multiple logistical responsibilities before the trip can even begin. They have every reason to assume that museum educators will understand the complexity they deal with. How often, however, have you heard a museum teacher complain that teachers on field trips are "taking a day off," that the museum is shouldering the burden of the experience alone? Far from neglecting her responsibilities, however, that weary classroom teacher has just undergone the many hassles of arguing for administrative permission for the trip, arranging all of the internal logistics, and tracking down each and every parent-signed permission slip. She has lined up chaperones, leased the buses, and survived the bus trip from the school to the museum. She may have had little time for the most elemental pre-visit preparations, despite the best of intentions. No wonder she is ready to let the museum teacher be the expert!

When museums and schools work together on setting goals and asking questions, they raise the odds for a successful experience. From the first phone call to a final evaluation, field trip planning is an exercise in good planning. Writing from the school perspective, administrator Fred Richter discussed the school's expectations of museums in the first edition of this book. Richter emphasized the importance of a positive experience, a visit that would result in students wanting to return. He noted that museums have the power to create the disposition to learn and that an experience of delight and pleasure should be a primary goal. He further noted, "A positive experience must *never* be sacrificed for the sake of adding more facts."[3]

Dr. Richter's advice was confirmed in a recent, two-year study in Cleveland.[4] The study involved 16 museums in the University Circle area of Cleveland and their school partners, including 28 schools and more than 600 K-8 classroom visits each year. Although teachers in the study cited multiple goals for their field trips, they related *affective* goals slightly higher than learning-related goals. The teachers consistently desired that students' experiences be highly positive and memorable. They acknowledged the need to tie museum visits to learning standards, but felt that the key to a successful field trip was giving students an exciting and rewarding experience. Once the student interest was aroused, the teachers felt far greater success in focusing on the factual and conceptual learning back in the classroom.

Logistics were the second concern of teachers surveyed back in 1989 and 1991, leading Dr. Richter to note that the best educational experience could be spoiled by poor planning. Once again, the Cleveland study confirmed this finding. Teachers wanted programs that ran like clockwork. They noted that learning declines with uncertainty about such things as arrival logistics, timing, lunch arrangements, and teachers' and chaperones' roles. A well thought-out and well executed game plan alleviates frustration and distraction, leaving full focus on the learning experience itself.

Despite a growing emphasis on the museum as a resource for learning, the idea of seeing "everything" on a field trip remains a difficult one to dissuade. Teachers often are expecting a full museum tour, taking students from gallery to gallery with little opportunity to look closely and carefully. The field trip as a "museum parade"—not unlike Holden Caulfield's experience described in the introduction—is a misuse of what should be a rich opportunity to experience one or two topics more fully. Once again, good communication is essential.

Field trip evaluations also reveal that students crave some freedom for their own explorations. Young people commonly report that they would rather visit a museum with their families than with a school group. Family visits are more likely to include time for students to explore on their own and make their own discoveries. As Fred Richter's surveys revealed, students disliked being rushed and "talked at" too much. Instead, they wanted some opportunity to choose among the many fascinating exhibits to build on their own personal learning. Research further confirms that students seek the pleasure of social learning by interacting with one another in museums. When given a say in their museum experience, planning aspects of their visit, selecting topics to be studied and working together in small groups, students respond with greater enthusiasm. Purpose, choice and ownership are tools that work especially well for older students.

Museum visits also should exploit the characteristics that set museums aside from classrooms. Forget the worksheets with fill-in-the-blanks. Give students assignments that require looking, questioning and discovering. Learning in museums should emphasize observation over language and investigation rather than telling. What better way to view three-dimensional artifacts than through the lens of comparison and contrast, description and analysis? Careful examination, classification and interpretation are the tools of critical thinking, a process that should be inspired and practiced in the museum setting and transferred back into the classroom.

Using critical thinking skills in the museum invites students to become more hands-on and engaged. They should be able to handle, manipulate, and examine some objects. Their experience should have a personal brand. Museums have unique opportunities to present multi-sensory learning and complement the text-bound learning of the classroom. Many students are not traditional learners, but come alive when they are asked to solve mysteries, touch objects, and move through exhibits and experiences in more physical and sensory-driven ways. These are the experiences that should fuel the imaginative teacher and museum educator, suggesting how to create multilayered ways of learning and address many different learning styles.

A Case to Consider

The following case study explores the essential question: What do museums and schools need to understand about one another to build sustainable and cogent partnerships? Mark D. Osterman's critical observations outline strategies and describe methods that he has employed to build sustained partnerships that are mutually beneficial and based in theory.

The Museums Magnet Program (MMP) brings together a series of schools and museums to extend learning beyond the school walls and into museums and cultural institutions. Key components of the program are ongoing learning expeditions where students have personal contact with authentic artifacts and works of art at various cultural institutions. These learning expeditions are integrated into the total school curriculum and typically involve planning and collaboration between teachers and museum educators. Museum educators also work collaboratively with classroom teachers throughout the year to develop specially designed thematic units that integrate the standards-driven curriculum with the objects, artifacts, and collections of their respective museums. This integrated curriculum, focusing primarily on object- and project-based learning, emphasizes communication, problem solving, exploration, inquiry and creativity.

By placing the object at the core of the learning process, students gain skills that are critical to all areas of learning. Objects provide a concrete experience that aids and illuminates abstract thought. Interest in them, and their power to motivate, is cumulative, so that as pupils learn, they put themselves in a position of wanting to learn more.[5] As students have personal contact with authentic objects in their classrooms, local neighborhoods, and museums, they also bring their own personal background and experiences into the learning process.

Professional development activities conducted for the MMP are based in constructivist theories and focus on facilitation, learner-centered practice, experiential learning and inquiry. The theory of constructivism promotes learning by doing and suggests that learners construct knowledge to become independent critical thinkers. Teachers play the role of facilitators allowing for open-ended outcomes. Interactions with objects, unlike many other mediators, allow constructivist notions of personal experience, interpretation, self-motivation, and critical thought to emerge. The MMP asks teachers to gain an understanding of constructivist pedagogies and apply them to object-based learning activities in the classroom and the museum.

This specialized partnership is funded by Miami–Dade County Public Schools through a three-year grant awarded by the U.S. Department of Education's Magnet Assistance Program. The grant money is used to get the program up and running. The school district continues providing extra funding for the magnet program once the grant funds have been exhausted, but this funding is well below the levels offered through the grant. It is during the grant period that schools and museums attempt to create sustained partnerships that represent collaboration not only of resources, but also of theory and practice.

What do museums and schools need to understand about one another to build sustainable and cogent partnerships? Experiences with the MMP reveal five areas of understanding. These should be viewed as mutual and can be used as a guide for developing sustained partnerships.

First, it is important for partners to understand each other's *profession* and its practitioners. When beginning the MMP, most teachers were not familiar with what museum educators do. It was necessary to have museum educators define their training, responsibilities, and range of work. Teachers often were unaware that museum educators had classroom experience and/or advanced degrees in education similar to their own. They further learned that both professions centered on the theories of cognitive development and other theoretical frameworks that guided practice. It was through open discourse and transparency in relation to practice that teachers and museum educators began to understand each other's profession.

Second, partners need to understand *values* that each are committed to in terms of their educational practice. Identifying these values helps initiate a dialogue that can further define future goals for partnerships. During the development stages of the MMP, museum partners recognized the importance of stating these values to school faculty. As a result, museum educators from The Historical Museum of Southern Florida, The Lowe Art Museum, University of Miami, The Miami Art Museum, and The Wolfsonian-FIU got together and crafted a list of values they wanted to bring to the partnership. Developing these values and then sharing them with school administration and faculty was illuminating for all, generating rich discussion, and serving as the seed for a shared sense of purpose. The museums' set of values included the following:

*museums serve as an extended classroom for students and teachers
*experiences incorporate inquiry-based teaching and learning methods
*objects and exhibitions are used to teach core disciplines
*content and methodologies are developmentally appropriate

*activities are experiential and/or project-based
*curriculum content recognizes standards-based learning
*professional development and collaboration with schools is a priority
*teaching methods are research-based and represent best practices

A good resource to help teachers understand museum education values is the American Association of Museums (AAM) document, "Characteristics of an Accreditable Museum," which states many of the core ideas related to education.[6]

Teachers also can explore AAM's "Excellence in Practice: Museum Education Principles and Standards,"[7] developed in 2002 to guide and inform the practice of museum education. By being aware of expected professional values and conventions for museum education practice, teachers can identify sets of values that correspond to their own. This will help establish a professional relationship where goals and expectations are clear.

Third, partners need to consider and understand the unique school and museum *environments* and the advantages and disadvantages each offers. It is best for teachers to view the museum as a laboratory for learning. Museum galleries and educational departments are not tied to standardized testing and school board restrictions. This allows for an educational environment of experimentation. The architecture of museums also plays a role in how learning takes place. While museum structures often inspire awe and curiosity, they can sometimes instill a sense of alienation and insecurity for many students, an issue that museums must take quite seriously. To break down possible barriers, museum educators need to collaborate with schools to give a voice to the students and to make the museum a place that invites wonder and discovery. By leaving a sense of mystery, the museum environment becomes an open vessel for students to consider. In his book, *The Promise of Cultural Institutions*, David Carr states that there is no comparable place—authoritative, venerable, reflective—for a thoughtful person to take a good question and work on it. And there is nowhere else where the inspiring traces of other questioning human beings are so clearly present.[8] The uniqueness of the museum's environment and its ability to instill a sense of inquiry are great tools for teachers and museum educators to encourage through facilitation. Part of the MMP placed an emphasis on affecting change within the school environment to mimic some aspects of museums and galleries. This was done through the installation throughout the school of artwork connected to curriculum, offering explicit and tacit learning opportunities for students and teachers as they walked the hallways.

Museum educators must be cognizant of how different the school environment is from the museum. Teachers must deal with many issues: the restrictions and pressures from standardized testing, classroom discipline, often unmotivated students, adversarial parents, and sometimes difficult working conditions with a lack of resources. Unless museum educators are empathetic to these issues, they discourage rich collaboration.

Fourth, partners need to understand the *theories* that inform each other's *practice*. In the MMP, museums based their practice in constructivist strategies when working with teachers and students. This required museums to explain the benefit of constructivist strategy in the context of museum-school collaborations. Through modeling, museum educators showed teachers that the incorporation of art and objects into the classroom naturally promoted constructivist strategies such as inquiry, student-centered practice and experiential learning. Hooper-Greenhill states that experiential learning is the process of creating and transforming experience into knowledge, skills, attitudes, values, emotions, beliefs, and senses. It is the process through which individuals become themselves.[9] For young children, much teaching is experiential and incorporates all of the senses. But as children progress through their school year, multi-modal teaching often yields to text-based teaching, relying on the word rather than experience to learn. The MMP attempted to rectify this by working with teachers in curriculum development to re-insert the arts into the teaching and learning process and make it more experiential. Only by clearly discussing theory and practice did collaborations germinate into rich interdisciplinary curricula.

Fifth, partners need to look at and understand *research* that each has conducted. Research represents rigorous, exploratory, and reflective practice and can be used as an advocacy tool. Partners always should consider if any new opportunities exist for formative and/or summative research when developing sustained partnerships. Teachers have the opportunity to conduct active research projects in collaboration with museum educators and together develop a research plan for the classroom setting. The MMP had a major research evaluation project attached to it that included teachers being trained on basic evaluation methods, rubric development, and data administration. The exposure to the research side of the partnership led some teachers into a self-initiated project to create new rubrics to evaluate student work as it specifically relates to object-based learning. This intriguing development became a new facet of collaboration between museum educators and teachers.

These five areas of understanding are essential to the development of strong teacher-school collaborations, transforming the informal "field trip" into something like a "learning expedition," a meaningful extension of the classroom experience. Teachers and museum educators must meet each other halfway; each must bend and take on a little of the other's role to empathize and understand what is really possible. The formation of a partnership signals the interest of both museum and school staff in collaborating on a long-term basis to achieve shared goals.[10] Clearly understanding one another can only lead toward real and sustained collaborations between schools and museums.

✳ ✳ ✳

NOTES

1. Beverly Sheppard, ed., *Building Museum and School Partnerships* (Harrisburg, PA: Pennsylvania Federation of Museums and Historical Organizations, 1993).

2. John H. Falk and Lynn D. Dierking, "Recalling the Museum Experience," *Journal of Museum Education* 20, no. 2 (1995): 10–13.

3. Fred Richter, *Building Museum and School Partnerships*, op cit., 10.

4. Unpublished. *Research study conducted by Institute for Learning Innovation*, 2005, 2006.

5. Gail Durbin, Susan Morris, Sue Wilkinson, *Learning From Objects* (United Kingdom: English Heritage, 1990), 1.

6. American Association of Museums, *Characteristics of an Accreditable Museum* (Washington D.C.: American Association of Museums, 2005).

7. American Association of Museums Education Committee, *Excellence in Practice: Museum Education Principles and Standards* (Washington. D.C.: American Association of Museums, 2002).

8. David Carr, *The Promise of Cultural Institutions* (New York: AltaMira Press, 2003), 94–95.

9. Eileen Hooper-Greenhill, "The Power of Museum Pedagogy" ed. Hugh H. Genoways, *Museum Philosophy for the 21st Century* (New York: AltaMira Press, 2006), 243.

10. Margaret K. Burchenal and Sara Lasser, "Beyond the Field Trip," ed. Pat Villeneuve, *From Periphery to Center: Art Museum Education in the 21st Century* (Reston, VA: National Art Education Association, 2007).

2

Meeting Teachers' Needs

Maria Marable-Bunch

The demands on the classroom teacher have become increasingly complex in the 21st century. This chapter underscores the art of listening to teachers' needs as the starting point for successful partnerships. As museums position themselves as resources for students and teachers, they need to start with understanding how and what to provide as support materials and services. Where to begin? Ask a teacher.

✳ ✳ ✳

Educators are always looking for good teaching materials and resources to enhance and bring their curriculum to life. Conscientious teachers fill their "instructional toolbox" with resources gathered from many sources, including museums. Museums are great resources because their unique learning experiences are built around the "real stuff"—the authentic materials that connect students to the world around them. Learning opportunities for teachers and school groups include an array of formats: curriculum materials, museum tours, teacher seminars and institutes, Internet resources, object kits, performances, and outreach activities in the schools. In recent years, museums have expanded their commitment to education even further, devoting more time to listening to and learning from classroom teachers, and engaging in deeper research to match their efforts to the greatest classroom needs. This is the essence of partnership.

With over 17,000 museums in this country, how does a teacher determine what museum resources to use in his or her classroom? Even more important, are museums at the top of the list of sources that teachers turn to for new instructional ideas and activities? Have museums earned the right and demonstrated the commitment to be on the top of this list? Have museums' efforts increased teachers' awareness, use, or appreciation of the services that museums offer to them and their students?

Today's teachers work in an increasingly complex and challenging environment. They face such extraordinary difficulties, such as overcrowded classrooms, limited support for "extracurricular activities," and the struggle to be innovative within the constrictions of "No Child Left Behind (NCLB)." Museums have both the opportunity and the responsibility to marshal their impressive resources and skills to help teachers do their jobs better and enhance the educational experiences of all students.

In order to understand the needs of teachers more fully, the author conducted research with 75 teachers representative of Pre-K through 12th grade across the country during the summer of 2009, requesting their responses to the following questions:

*What compels teachers to look beyond the classroom to enrich their curriculum?

*What criteria do teachers use to determine what resources to use?

*Does technology play a role in determining what is useful?

*What challenges do teachers face in accessing museum resources?

*What do teachers want museums to know about them, and how can museums contribute to the teachers' work in an age of high accountability and teacher scrutiny?

In response to what compels them to look beyond the classroom, one teacher replied, "I have always believed that the world is a classroom. To get students excited about learning takes many forms of media. The textbook can't even touch what is needed to make lessons relevant to students' lives or to their learning."[1] Another teacher indicated that she goes beyond her classroom for materials "to find inspiration, ideas, and information for lesson plans. Often, museum resources will offer innovative or unexpected ways to use objects in the classroom."[2] The overall responses indicated that teachers are always looking for new ideas and ways of doing things that will enable them to vary their teaching strategies and ensure they are offering a range of activities that address the different learning styles of their students.

Teachers use a range of criteria when looking for useful resource materials. Familiarity ranked high on the survey, which noted that teachers who had been invited to collaborate with museum educators on resource development were more inclined to use the product. They were familiar with its content and knew how it would mesh with their lesson plans. Ease of access to resources was also cited as important. "Having resources readily and easily available on a website certainly helps to access information"[3] was the response of a teacher who searches the Internet frequently. Another teacher went on to say, "I personally am drawn to resources that are interesting to me and offer fresh and clever ways to integrate the arts into my curriculum."[4]

When the objectives and expected outcomes of museum resources mirror academic standards, curricula requirements, and skill-building activities, they are more likely to be used in the classroom. A former principal of a museum magnet school in Washington, D.C. said she looked at standards first and then matched the resources to the curriculum. She noted, "Museums present the opportunity for students to build skills in research and analysis of data. The encounter is also an opportunity to use technology. Most of the students are technologically savvy and if you don't involve it [technology], then students will become disinterested . . . Research is the main area in which I like to see students involved."[5]

Connection to standards, student learning styles, and teacher interests often drive how resources are prioritized. For example, an art teacher said that she is not always concerned with the art history or factual information, but instead appreciates examples of ways to lead discussions, provide questions to ask her students, and create solid educational activities to do with students. Other teachers said that they download images of objects or works of art to create bulletin boards or to prompt discussions. Teachers noted that they used museum loan kits or trunks in the classroom or in the museum when the kits included materials for students' direct use and targeted a specific discipline.

Learning resources continue to be essential when the students visit the museum. Teachers reported that they look for pre-visit materials to prepare their students for an upcoming museum experience. However, some indicated that hands-on training or a personal introduction to the museum by museum educators helped them become better acquainted with the museum's environment. Such an approach also helped them understand how to incorporate the resources into their teaching and thus better prepare their students for the museum experience. With such exposure, teachers said that they were more likely to plan a museum visit for their students.

Many teachers stressed the need to build a comfort level for teachers using museums. To do so, museum educators must network diligently with teachers and administrators to provide access, skills and understanding of how to use museums. The teachers also expressed the need for museum educators to know and understand the climate of the classroom.

The No Child Left Behind Act (NCLB), the 2001 law that imposed stronger accountability in student academic achievement and teacher performance, had an unintended consequence for museum-school partnerships. It forced teachers to turn away from museums at the very time when museums could have played an important role in improving academic achievement. NCLB challenged museum educators to rethink their institutions' educational products for the teacher and school group audiences.

The impact of school reform law was immediately felt on one of the field's most stable programs—the field trip. A recent edition of the *Journal of Museum Education* (*The Field Trip: Enigma or Paradigm*)[6] featured an article about the evolution of school trip programs at the Japanese American National Museum and what its educators learned in a collaborative effort with teachers to restructure its programs. The museum's educators heard that" . . . . in the future teachers must more carefully monitor four aspects of field trip topics: purpose, student performance, preparation, and support. If teachers need to examine these areas, then museums must as well. What content standards does the museum trip address? How will students demonstrate proficiency after their visits? Are students able to synthesize their experience in a meaningful way? What can museum staff do to support teacher work?" Clearly, all of a museum's teaching resources must be examined for their usefulness, relevance, and support of academic goals.

As a result of all this self-analysis, museum and school partnerships have had to rethink the word "relevance." Museum educators today must review program offerings, and carefully study and make connections to national, state and local academic standards. The goal is to ensure that museum resources support the changes in classroom instruction and professional development for teachers. The connection to standards is essential for all kinds of museum programs: distance learning, outreach programs, professional development for teachers, lesson plans on the web, publications, and school group tours and activities. Museum educators increasingly study and apply Pre-Kindergarten-12 educational practices in learning theories, teaching methods, and curriculum designs.

The emphasis on relevance has created a major paradigm shift in museum education practices as museums place more emphasis on deeply understanding the challenges and needs of teachers in today's education system. It has helped museums discover how they as learning entities can play a major role in and influence educational reform.

Museums are offering an increased level of services and programs to teachers that are thoughtful and relevant to student needs. Collaboration has led to museum-provided resources and services that contribute to increased academic achievement in students. For example, museum educators at the Art Institute of Chicago were informed by a Chicago Public School art educator that the State of Illinois standardized test included samples of works of art from the museum's collection to measure students' knowledge of art terms, artists, and art appreciation. Staff immediately saw this as an opportunity to create a program that would help art teachers prepare their students. The AIC staff produced a teacher professional development workshop that addressed the works of art featured and helped teachers determine how to integrate teaching about the elements of art, the making of art and art history in preparing students for the exam. The museum invited its advisory panel of educators to help structure the content of the workshop as well as serve as teacher instructors for the implementation of the program. The panel of educators' "real world" knowledge enriched the museum's offering in a way that enabled the museum to be seen as central rather than ancillary. As a follow-up to the workshop, participating teachers shared the lesson plans and activity ideas they used in their classroom as a result of the program. These ideas were then posted on the museum's website as a resource for other teachers.

In another unique school and museum partnership, the State of Illinois and the Chicago Board of Education have become leaders in recognizing museums as an integral part of students' educational experiences. Chicago Public Schools and nine Chicago area museums[7] partnered to create curricula that integrated the Chicago area museums' resources with the Chicago Academic Standards through the development of comprehensive thematic units. The project, *Museums and Public Schools*, consisted of curriculum units of ideas and lessons. The curricula included teacher resource guides and student workbooks. A design team composed of Chicago Public Schools teachers and museum educators worked together to create teacher- and student-friendly lessons, based on the Illinois State Goals and Learning Standards. Five fundamental areas—Language Arts, Mathematics, Science, Social Science and Fine Arts—became the foundation of each integrated lesson.[8]

Considering all of the efforts of museum educators to provide the best and most useful educational services for teachers, another question was posed to the surveyed teachers: What hinders them from accessing this vast wealth of information and programs? A former principal commented on the challenges of accessing museum resources, "It can be time-consuming. However, the more museum resources reflect standards and their local school district curriculum requirements, the easier it is for a teacher to incorporate them into lesson plans . . . Most administrators do not understand the value of museums. If museum resources are not addressed in state assessment, then they will not be addressed at all in the classroom. Teachers need meaningful alignment with standards and existing curricula and the resources should help alleviate the work of planning, not make more work."[9] All the teachers concluded that if a program successfully enhances higher academic achievement and accountability of teacher performances, the teacher will be more likely to take advantage of museum resources.

Putting It Into Practice

To guarantee that your resources and programs are beneficial to teachers in the classroom, museum educators should consider the following actions:

1. Deepen your understanding of a familiar but ever-changing audience. Make sure that museums recognize that the best museum educators are conversant with the important current concerns of the American education system. This understanding is accomplished only by a willingness to navigate deeper into the world of the education system.

*Involve teachers as well as school administrators from every level in planning, implementation, and assessing the results.

*Stay abreast of educational reform by attending educators' professional annual conferences like the Association of Supervision and Curriculum Development, National Art Education Association, or the National Council of Social Studies.

*Visit schools to better understand the "Life of a Teacher."

*Incorporate activities—within resources and programming—that engage students in making meaningful connections to their lives.

2. Cultivate advocates in the public education field. Museum educators need to push harder to be at the table with the policy makers and become more visible as a valuable resource. When you consider, collectively, how museums' resources—well researched and designed, often with teacher input—complement and enrich classroom instruction, museums can no longer stand around, waiting for recognition. Getting involved in the national discussion and decision-making could be the next revolution in museum education. *Museums must find a way to be on the agenda of such national organizations as the United States Department of Education, the National Education Association or the Council of Chief State Education Officers to give input and shape policies stressing the importance of learning using museum resources.*Don't overlook the board of education members in local districts, as well as superintendents of state education departments, who may serve as advocates in their school districts for the inclusion of museum resources in district and state standard-based curricula.

3. Offer teacher-centered resources and programs that are hard to resist.

*Museum educators must open the door wider for inclusion, thus lessening the burden for teachers to demonstrate that museum resources are the tools that matter most in their toolbox.

*Be an effective collaborator with teachers, demonstrating how museums can truly be of educational value.

*Create programs that assist teachers and students in reaching their educational goals.

With the implementation of these action ideas, maybe museums can finally be at the top of the list of most-needed educational tools for successful learning and teaching in the classroom.

NOTES

1. Lynne Long, Ed.D., former museum school principal and professional development specialist, Washington, D.C., response to survey by author, 24 August 2009.

2. Tanya Brown-Merriman, former teacher (Art Education) and museum educator, Los Angeles, Calif., response to survey by author and interview by author, 21 August 2009.

3. Rita Johnson, Principal, Nannie Helen Burroughs Elementary School, Washington, D.C., telephone interview by author, 8 June 2009.

4. Brown-Merriman, survey response and interview.

5. Long, survey response.

6. *Journal of Museum Education* 30, nos. 2 and 3 (Fall 2005): 6.

7. The nine museums: The Art Institute of Chicago, Chicago Children's Museum, Chicago History Museum, DuSable Museum of African American History, The National Museum of Mexican Fine Arts, John G. Shedd Aquarium, Museum of Science and Industry, Peggy Notebaert Nature Museum of the Chicago Academy of Sciences, and The Field Museum.

8. *Museums and Public Schools Curriculum Project (MAPS)*, Chicago Public Schools and the City of Chicago, 2003.

9. Long, survey response.

3

Schools in the 21st Century

Kathrine Walker Schlageck

Twenty-first century schools have changed a lot since the 1993 publication of the first edition of *Building Museum and School Partnerships*. The differences that have emerged in these 17 years present both challenges and opportunities for museums and great potential for museums and schools to work together toward common goals. This chapter describes the realities of schools in the 21st century, including the uses of new and innovative technologies, and speculates on continuing trends and possible changes.

✳ ✳ ✳

No Child Left Behind

The passage of No Child Left Behind (NCLB) in 2001, with heavy emphasis on testing, has wrought some of the most dramatic change in the 21st-century classroom. Even private schools and home schools, which are not required to participate in yearly testing, are aware that their students will need to meet similar goals to be competitive. While changes will be made to NCLB in the coming years, it is highly likely that accountability based on performance will continue in some form.

NCLB places an increased emphasis on math and language arts and decreased emphasis on social studies, sciences, foreign languages, and the arts. A 2007 Center on Education Policy report stated that 62% of school districts reported increasing the time spent on math and language arts and 44% reported cutting time from other subjects.[1] Social studies was cut by an average of 76 minutes, science by an average of 75 minutes, and art and music by an average of 57 minutes per week.[2]

Numerous articles and reports also outline the impact of NCLB on museums. Classroom teachers surveyed by the Smithsonian in 2007 indicated that NCLB has changed the way they teach, including the administration mandating that they teach to the test, merely highlight state standards, and spend less time on in-depth study or revisiting a topic.[3] A 2009 American Association of Museums' Annual Meeting roundtable and a 2008 attitude study by the Midwest Museums Association summarized implications of testing on field trips.

> *The period of several weeks to two or three months before and during testing is blacked out by schools for field trips.
>
> *Testing is not always scheduled at the beginning of the school year and teachers have to cancel pre-arranged field trips once the schedule is announced.

*Some schools allow field trips only after testing is complete in an effort to keep students "on task."

Funds that were formerly used for field trips are now used for remediating students.[4]

Finally, NCLB initiatives have not been adequately funded, resulting in school dollars often being redistributed toward accountability rather than enrichment. Beth Nietzel, an eighth-grade teacher said, "Since the field trip budget comes from building funds, and districts are reprioritizing budgets, funding is not always available even if a great opportunity presents itself. Our recent excursion to the art museum would not have occurred had there not been a grant that could pay for the transportation."[5]

Museums are responding to NCLB by:

*targeting grade levels to correspond to test schedules, e.g., clustering third- to sixth-grade level tours in the fall or late spring, and second-grade and below between January and April;

*integrating more math and language arts into programs;[6]

*establishing advisory committees of stakeholders from public, private, and home schools that will help identify connections between NCLB mandates and museum collections and program possibilities;

*demonstrating the connections that the museum makes to desired NCLB skills and marketing these connections in promotional materials and workshops; and

*reviewing fees charged to schools for field trips and pursuing outside support for tours and buses.

Academic Standards

Often tied to, and sometimes confused with, NCLB is an increased emphasis on academic standards, with states developing their own standards and benchmarks in addition to the national standards that have been put forth by professional associations. Local districts utilize and integrate standards in all manner of ways, but they typically use a mix of national, state and local standards. In a recent report entitled "Classroom Realities" from the Smithsonian Institution Office of Policy and Analysis, about 69% of surveyed teachers use a history curriculum designed to meet state standards, while only 7% teach to national standards and 8% to local or district standards.[7] This may change as the political winds blow one way or the other; currently 47 states are working together to develop a better set of national standards to replace individual state standards.

Standards and benchmarks can be a useful guide for museums, especially since teachers report that field trips and other programs with external parties are approved based on how well standards are met. Museums are responding to the increasing role of education standards by:

*considering the widest net of content area standards that apply and finding concrete demonstrable programmatic examples;

*developing and testing programs with local teachers to ensure curricular fit; and

*marketing the relevance of programs to the standards.

Technology in the Classroom

The use of new technologies also has had a dramatic impact on teaching and learning. The incorporation of technology-driven teaching materials may be the most striking difference between the 21st-century classroom and its 20th-century counterpart, and change is continually underway. A 2008 Smithsonian survey of teachers indicated that 84% have computers less than 5 years old, while 90% have Internet access, projection equipment and white boards, and more than 90% download classroom materials. Teachers reported that materials, with curricula/lesson plans timed to class period length (50 minutes average) were in the highest demand. The use of primary source materials, available through the Internet, and distance learning opportunities followed. There also was a need indicated for non-English materials, especially Spanish.[8] In addition, classrooms are utilizing podcasts, cell phone connections, audio and video distance learning, live chats and other tools for the delivery and application of content.

For many museums, technology may be one of the best and most cost-effective ways to serve teachers and schools. Erika Sanger, director of education at the Albany Institute of History and Art, said, "As we have seen our school and teacher program attendance decline by 10% a year over the past two years because of school district budget restrictions, our programs delivered through technology, including on-line lessons and video-conferencing, have grown at a steady 7–10% annually."[9]

The uses of technology to support museum and school programming are still being tested and evaluated. A full summary of new programming of this sort would require more space than is available in this chapter. Some might even be nearly obsolete by the time of publication. Nonetheless, a few guidelines are necessary. Using technology should be considered in the same way that other interpretive and educational strategies are employed, by selecting the right tool for the task and beginning the planning with the end in mind. As with any type of delivery mechanism, the first question to resolve is "Who is the audience for this program?" and then fit the technology to the audience and learning goals.

Looking across the span of even the most recent technologies, one quickly sees a breadth of possibilities. These include a variety of social networking tools, from Facebook to Twitter. There are collaboration tools, such as blogs and wikis, which could be compelling places for school groups to undertake problem-solving. There are an increasing number of online gaming sites, including ones that engage multiple players. Technology provides for widespread delivery of teaching materials and teaching forums, such as webinars, and has enormous capabilities for students and teachers to assemble their own materials from multiple sites. Add mobile technologies to the list, a growing focus on mixed and augmented realities, and the host of online digital resources, and the learning possibilities continue to grow. Some of these tools focus on the single user, while others maximize group learning and exploration. Increasingly, frameworks for co-design, participatory, and user-centered design, even with young children, are undergoing testing and experimentation. Ultimately determining the delivery mechanisms for learning partnerships depends on a careful analysis of at least three factors:

*the goals of the learning program;

*access to the tools of technology; and

*individual skill in developing and using the tools.

Although the "digital divide" of access is shrinking, it is not gone and must be considered when designing programs that will reach all intended audiences.

New Variations on Traditional Issues Impacting Museum Programs for Schools

For decades museum educators have been keeping up with the challenges that teachers face in paying for external programs and carving time out of a packed school day. Museum educators know, for example, that they must learn everything they can about the curriculum of targeted schools and that they must be able to demonstrate the relevance of their programs to the curriculum. But economic woes and high-stakes testing bring new challenges including:

*the lack of funds for program fees, transportation, and substitutes;

*larger class sizes due to teacher lay-offs, exacerbating teachers' concerns about logistics and behavioral issues on field trips; and

*a much tighter school day with little to no time for anything not viewed as directly relevant to benchmarks and testing.

*Museums have responded to these new twists on traditional concerns by:

*increasing the number and availability of programs brought to the classroom by museum staff;

*working with teacher advisory committees to develop testing prompts utilizing museum content; and

*demonstrating an understanding of the challenges that teachers face by providing ready-to-use curriculum materials.

Teachers still report the importance of field trips, however. Kari Kufahl, an elementary school teacher, said, "Our district has always believed that 'being-there experiences' are best. With no art specialist in our school, it is extremely valuable every time we visit the art museum. The hands-on projects are always a favorite and help 'cement' learning."[10]

Opportunities in Early Childhood Education

Museums, with their emphasis on gaining knowledge through hands-on learning and the development of cognitive and communication skills, are well suited to serve younger learners.

Funding for early education initiatives continues to grow, with $2 billion in extra stimulus money in 2010 for Early Start, Head Start, and Even Start. Federal Acts 62 and 132 have provided funding for pre-kindergarten programs since 2007. In addition, the 2010 U.S. Department of Education budget request includes $500 million for new Title 1 early childhood programs, $300 million in Early Childhood Learning Challenge Funds, and $162.5 million for Early Reading First.[11] Full-day kindergarten programs also are on the rise.

Children's museums and exploration centers, in particular, are responding to opportunities in early childhood education. Some resources to note:

Association of Children's Museums (www.childrensmuseums.org);

Smithsonian Early Enrichment Center (www.seec.si.edu);

*"The Museum and Me: An Early Childhood Art Education Model," Claire Schaefer and Elizabeth Cole (Toledo Museum of Art), ERIC ED343721, December 1990;

*"Young Children's Perspectives and Museum Settings and Experiences," Barbara Piscitelli and David Anderson, Museum Management and Curatorship 19, issue 3, September 2001, 269–282; and

*Headstart and the National Endowment for the Humanities' early childhood version of "Picturing America" (www.eclkc.ohs.acf.hhs.gov/hslc/resources/cinema/Vid/19444test.pdf).

After-School Programs

The U.S. Department of Education reported in 2008 that 56% of schools sponsor one or more types of after-school programs, serving four million children.[12] Since most of these programs stress enrichment opportunities for children, museums are natural partners. The following are useful resources:

*Communities in Schools: After-School Program Toolkit (www.cisnet.org/working_together/after-school.asp);

*National Institute of Out Of School Time (www.NIOST.org);

*Service organizations, including the Boys and Girls Club of America (www.bgca.org) and YMCA (www.ymca.net); and

*The Department of Education funds 21st-Century Community Learning Centers (www.ed.gov/programs/21stcclc/index.html).[13]

Charter and Magnet Schools

Charter schools are increasingly taking root in communities across the country. Museums should become acquainted with the charter schools in their target area, find out why and how they were founded, and determine points of juncture with their philosophies of education. Resources for learning about charter schools include:

*The U.S. Department of Education (www.ed.gov/programs/charter);

*The National Association of Charter School Authorizers (www.qualitycharters.org);

*The National Alliance for Public Charter Schools (www.publiccharters.org); and

*The American Association of Museums (www.aam-us.org/pubs/mn/MN_SO98_MuseumCharter.cfm).

Magnet schools provide focused educational programs, such as in math or science. Many museums, including the Smithsonian, the Brooklyn Museum of Art, and the Franklin Institute, provide rich resources for partnering with magnet schools. More information is available from Magnet Schools of America at http://www.magnet.edu/.

21st-Century Skills

"I'm calling on our nation's governors and state education chiefs to develop standards and assessments that don't simply measure whether students can fill in a bubble on a test, but whether they possess 21st-century skills like problem-solving and critical thinking and entrepreneurship and creativity."
—*Barack Obama*[14]

"The Museums, Libraries and 21st-Century Skills" initiative from the Institute of Museum and Library Services (IMLS) underscores the critical role our nation's libraries and museums play in helping citizens build needed skills such as information, communications and technology literacy, critical thinking, problem solving, creativity, civic literacy, and global awareness. The website at www.imls.gov/about/21CSkills/shtm#about includes three components:

*a report outlining the role of libraries and museums in the national dialogue around learning and 21st-century skills;
*a self-assessment tool to help institutions determine where they fit on the continuum of 21st-century skills; and
*an online self-assessment offering a quick survey to analyze an institution's 21st-century strategies.

A separate program, the Partnership for 21st-Century Learning Skills (P21) consists of 13 pilot states. Museums are uniquely suited to address a number of the identified skills, including scientific, visual and cultural literacy; global awareness; curiosity, creativity and risk-taking; higher-order thinking skills and sound reasoning; teaming and collaborative learning; and interactive communication. Curriculum maps for the subject areas of geography, math, language arts, science and social studies are available on the P21 website, http://www.21stcenturyskills.org, under resources.

Political Initiatives

It is a safe bet that presidential administrations and the U.S. Congress will take positions on education policy for decades to come, developing requirements and new initiatives designed to tackle the problems of the moment. Museums will do well to stay informed about the prevailing political winds so that they can develop and/or tweak programs in accordance with new requirements or funding initiatives. They will do even better by finding a seat at the table in order to be a part of the conversation before new policies are written.

Putting It Into Practice

Schools are changing rapidly. Consider these tips to staying current:

*establish and maintain relationships with local educators, and listen closely to them to understand their concerns and challenges;

*keep track of changes in curriculum, standards, and testing schedules;

*consider private schools, home schools, charter schools and magnet schools when developing program ideas;

*pursue collaborations with schools that are seeking federal funds;

*explore early childhood and after/summer school audiences;

*follow advances in technology; experiment and pursue opportunities in technology with schools; and

*think carefully about 21st-century skills and articulate your institution's unique position to provide schools with innovative hands-on learning laboratories for creative and critical thinking and better global understanding.

NOTES

1. Jennifer McMurrer, "Choices, Changes, and Challenges: Curriculum and Instruction in the NCLB Era," *From the Capitol to the Classroom: Year 5 of the No Child Left Behind Act*, revised December 2007. (Washington, D.C.: Center for Education Policy. 2007): 1. http://www.cep-dc.org/_data/n_0001/resources/live/07107%20Curriculum-WEB%20FINAL%207%2031%2007.pdf.

2. Jennifer McMurrer, "Instructional Time in Elementary Schools: A Closer Look at Changes for Specific Subjects," *From the Capitol to the Classroom: Year 5 of the No Child Left Behind Act*. (Washington, D.C.: Center on Education Policy, February 2008): 1-2 http://www.cep-dc.org/index.cfm?fuseaction=document.showDocumentByID&nodeID=1&DocumentID=234.

3. "Classroom Realities: Results of the 2007 National Survey of Teachers," (Washington, D.C.: Smithsonian Institution Office of Policy & Analysis and the National Museum of American History, April 2008): 6. http://www.museum-ed.org/images/stories/classroom_realities.pdf.

4. "Notes from 2009 AAM Roundtable on School Programs," Museum-ed website. www.museum-ed.org/content/view/103/104 (Teacher Resources) and "No Child Left Behind Attitude Survey Results, 1/7/2008-3/1/2008," Education Committee of the Association of Midwest Museums, http://www.midwestmuseums.org.

5. Beth Nietzel, Teacher, Anthony Middle School, 383 District, Manhattan, Kansas, interview by author, 21 May 2009.

6. Teachers praised a reading/language arts curriculum from the National Museum of American History based on stories from American history. The Smithsonian Education Center provides examples of lesson plans and field trips responding to core subjects: www.smithsonianeducation.org.

7. "Classroom Realities: Results of the 2007 National Survey of Teachers,": 6.

8. "Classroom Realities: Results of the 2007 National Survey of Teachers,": 7, 8 and 17.

9. Erika Sanger, Director of Education at the Albany Institute of History, Albany, NY, interview by author, 10 July 2009.

10. Kari Kufahl, Teacher, Westmoreland Elementary School, 323 District, Westmoreland, KS, interview by author, 10 June 2009.

11. U.S. Department of Education, Budget Summary Fiscal Year 2010, Elementary and Secondary

Education (7 May 2009). http://www.ed.gov/about/overview/budget/budget10/summary/edlite-section3a.html.

12. Basmat Parsad and Laurie Lewis, "After-School Programs in Public Elementary Schools: First Look," (NCES 2009-043) National Center for Education Statistics, Institute of Education Sciences, U.S. Department of Education (February 2009): 2. http://nces.ed.gov/pubsearch/pubsinfo.asp?pubid=2009043.

13. U.S. Department of Education, Budget Summary Fiscal Year 2010, Elementary and Secondary Education (7 May 2009). http://www.ed.gov/about/overview/budget/budget10/summary/edlite-section3a.html.

14. Barack Obama, Remarks on Education to the Hispanic Chamber of Commerce, CBS News website (10 March 2009). www.nytimes.com/2009/03/10/us/politics/10text-obama.html.

4

Learning Theory in the Museum Setting

Beth A. Twiss Houting, Mary Jane Taylor, and Susy Watts

This chapter provides an introduction to some of the key learning theories that have guided and influenced museum and classroom education. Particular attention is focused on learning theories that pertain to settings where learners encounter "real" objects. The aim is to help educators think critically about the underpinnings of their instructional strategies, and to provide a shared vocabulary about learning theory to use when talking with classroom teachers.

✳ ✳ ✳

The education world is teeming with theoretical frameworks for how people learn. For museum educators creating museum-school partnerships, it can be valuable to grasp the commonalities and distinctions of each theory and how to apply or adapt these ideas to their work. There is also much about learning that museum educators know from their practice and research. We know that people learn from and with objects; we know that people create their own learning.

This chapter examines the major learning theories cited by many museum educators. It is by no means exhaustive; it is intended to foster exploration of this challenging topic.

Why Theory?

Why should museum educators care to articulate the learning theory behind their programs? Theory substantiates the value of programs to educators and funders. Classroom educators seek proven work, not just "show and tell" examples of teaching. Increasingly rare is the casual field trip to the museum; teachers and students are coming to the museum with purpose. Funders want to be assured that their investment will have the highest possible pay-off.

Theory substantiates why and how learning occurs by identifying the attributes that assure successful learning. Theories that are field-tested and vetted by other educators show that a successful educational encounter can be repeated in different disciplines, contexts and cultures, and over the course of time. Just like classroom teachers, museum educators can isolate the successful attributes of teaching strategies. This allows museum educators to say more assuredly that a selected teaching process will contribute to learning, whether using a theory developed within a school or one suggested by museum work. Theories become not only explanations, but ideas or principles for ways to work.

Fortunately, school and museum educators seem to understand the same fundamental concepts about learning. Much of education philosophy in schools and museums today is based upon the theory of constructivism, that is, learners construct knowledge for themselves individually and/or socially as they learn. In teaching, the focus changes from being about a specific subject to being about the way individuals think about their learning and how their experiences in the moment affect the meaning they make.[1] Popular educational phrases for this theory are "differentiated learning" and "meaning making."

Practitioners from the two arenas of school and museum education, however, sometimes are challenged by these semantics. For example, classroom teachers utilize theories from bodies of research on topics as diverse as after-school and family learning,[2] teacher coaching models,[3] strategies for side-by-side teacher and student capacity-building,[4] habits of mind,[5] dispositions of successful learners,[6] and learning strategies for at-risk learners. They learn about these theories of learning by attending regional and national conferences, conducting web searches, and more often than not, following the advice of a successful colleague.

To overcome potential miscommunication and to better understand what classroom teachers are talking about, museum educators can read these theories and ponder their relevance to museum programming. Museum educators also can work side by side with teachers to follow the changing learning climate in the classroom and track the changes in educational theories over time. The next section of this chapter, along with the Education Theory Bookshelf, provides an overview of current theories.[7]

Learning Theories in Formal Education

Formal education in the United States owes much to the writings of American philosopher and educational reformer John Dewey. He was one of the earliest to espouse the core ideas of constructivism, believing learners construct knowledge for themselves as they learn. As a proponent of Pragmatism, Dewey held that knowledge is created when learners adapt to their environment what they gain from challenging and stimulating experiences. Children, in his view, were not empty vessels to be filled with knowledge, and schools needed to engage students in active learning.

Since then, theorists have focused on the characteristics of the learner and on the contexts that make learning possible. Some of these researchers have developed systems for classifying people by these characteristics, and others have given more consideration to the contexts in which the student learns.[8] Jean Piaget, Bernice McCarthy, and Howard Gardner are some of the well-known theorists in the first camp, creating systems for how people process information. Lev Vygotsy, Mikayli Csikszentmihayli, and John Keller on the other hand, look more at how the environment or conditions in which people learn affect the process.

Theories Focused on How People Process Information
Swiss developmental psychologist Jean Piaget devised a model of how children's learning naturally progresses through four stages of increasingly sophisticated cognitive development. Children move through this hierarchy as they age, he argued, building upon their

existing "mind maps" to understand the world. From the sensory-motor stage at birth, children grow into the preoperational and concrete operational stages of preschool and elementary school, which depend upon the presence of tangible objects to support learning. Abstract reasoning is a skill developed in later adolescence. In the 1970s and 80s, Piaget's theory underpinned a movement in American education to make instruction more child-centered. These same ideas greatly influenced the development of children's museums.

Bernice McCarthy's 4MAT system, one commonly adopted by educators in schools and museums, advances four primary learning styles to describe how individuals prefer to process information. Some work more abstractly, others work concretely; in addition, people tend to process information either reflectively or actively. She identifies the following styles:

*Innovative—the learner who observes and personalizes;

*Common Sense—the learner who tries things out first through exploration;

*Dynamic—the learner who designs new applications and examples and takes the extra step; and

*Analytic—the learner who learns by gathering information, reading and research.

In 1983, Harvard education professor Howard Gardner questioned the notion that children's abilities develop in a straightforward fashion. He outlined a contrasting theory of humans possessing multiple intelligences. Heavily influential in museum circles, Gardner described seven intelligences in his book *Frames of Mind:* linguistic, mathematical, musical, spatial, kinesthetic, interpersonal and intrapersonal. Today he continues to add to this list, including spiritual, moral, existential, and naturalist intelligences.

Two other theorists provide fodder for museum programs. In art education, Viktor Lowenfeld's analysis of children's drawings identified common, hierarchical stages of artistic development. In his 1947 book *Creative and Mental Growth*, he wrote about the social, aesthetic, intellectual and emotional growth in the art of children. Children, he observed, move from making scribbles at age two or three to producing highly realistic, representational drawings in their early teenage years. His stages of artistic development continue to help us understand how children see, respond to, and make images—skills that are analogous to learning from objects.

Edmund Feldman's visual analysis theories also apply to the process of looking critically. He identified two objective processes: Description (taking an inventory) and Analysis (thinking about the critical decisions that makers of objects consider). From this base, he suggests that learners move into the more subjective processes of Interpretation and Judgment. Viewers consider the formal properties, expressive properties and instrumental properties of objects and construct meaning.

Theories Focused on How Environment Affects Learning

While heavily influenced by Piaget, the theory of Russian psychologist Lev Vygotsky stresses the context beyond the individual. He found that learning happens within the everyday social interactions that children have with the people, objects, and events in their environments. While talking and playing with children, adult caregivers unconsciously teach the conventions of their culture. Vygotsky also argued that these adult-child interactions promote learning, as parents adjust their discussions to challenge their child to a level just beyond his or her previous understanding. He coined the term "zone of proximal development" to describe the learning that children can achieve with the help of a skilled and caring teacher—or in a museum with a guide or a label.

Theorists Mikayli Csikszentmihayli and John Keller also looked at context to understand the role of a challenging environment, which for some children could be a museum. Csikszentmihayli linked learning to situations where people are challenged just beyond their usual experience or ability. When a balance is struck between a person's skill, motivation and the task at hand, and when he becomes fully absorbed in what he is doing, he experiences a satisfying state Csikszentmihayli called "flow." For these learners, time, space, everyday concerns—even a sense of self—simply melt away. Keller, drawing upon research into the amount of effort a person is willing to exert in pursuit of a goal, argued that by understanding the four components of motivation (attention, relevance, confidence and satisfaction), educators can tailor teaching to student needs and provide appropriate levels of challenge.

Learning Theories from Museums

After almost half a century of visitor studies in museum settings, museum researchers and practitioners have theorized about visitor learning too. While learning is not the goal of each visitor to a museum, neither is learning the sole vision of each museum.[9] Still, affective and cognitive changes can be observed with most visitors. These changes can be defined by current neuroscience as learning, that is, neurons fire and memories and meanings are made.[10] Though some of the museum research has been undertaken with school children, most has been done with the general adult and family audience. The findings, nonetheless, influence work with children in museums and, in some ways, parallel and support traditional educational psychology.

One important way in which these studies are particularly useful for developing museum-school partnership programs is their emphasis on how people learn from objects, a primal way that humans learn[11] and the foundation for museum education.[12] One set of museum researchers, like educational theorists, identifies qualities within visitors that may affect how people learn in the museum environment, while another considers context.

Based upon extensive visitor research done with adult art museum visitors, the Denver Art Museum described visitors as either "novices" or "advanced amateurs,"[13] similar to the hierarchical systems laid out by Piaget and Lowenfeld. Novices have moderate to high interest in a subject but low to moderate knowledge, while the advanced amateurs have a higher knowledge base. Novices look for a positive experience where they see and emotionally experience something new, particularly while visiting with others. Advanced amateurs more often are interested in content rather than experience, often planning their visit in advance and spending more time in visual inspection of the art or object.

By contrast, when educators at Winterthur conducted research with people from age five to 95, they created a model more similar to Gardner's. The study examined the ways in which visitors innately thought about decorative arts or historic objects.[14] Because age and prior knowledge did not seem to affect visitors' thinking strategies after the age of seven, the categories were not seen as hierarchical, like Denver's two. Instead the responses were compared to a circle where visitors might utilize four different thinking strategies at varying points in their visit. A majority of people began by associating the object with a person in the present or the past. Other visitors, however, began by describing the physical characteristics of the object or classifying the object into categories, such as style periods or function. A fourth group judged or evaluated the object aesthetically or monetarily. Some visitors, on their own, utilized multiple strategies during the course of a response, but others benefited from modeling provided by a label or a guide.

Study of museum visitors' interactions with objects also supports constructivist theory in acknowledging highly personal outcomes. The Center for Learning In Out-of-School Environments at the University of Pittsburgh tries to define learning in "informal" settings, such as museums. In their work they determined that the use of objects or artifacts themselves categorize the learning that occurs in museums differently from that in classrooms, libraries, or other educational settings.[15] It is a more primal form of learning than from books, for example, as human beings understand how to learn from objects as soon as they begin to see.[16] In addition, these objects are presented in a designed environment that alters the physical context for learning.

The effect of physical context of the museum setting is of particular importance in designing museum-school programs. Museum researchers in the Philadelphia/Camden Informal Science Education Collaborative posited that by studying how people engage with exhibits, they can use observed behavior to determine if learning has occurred. In its study, families learn more from exhibits that are multi-sided, multi-modal, intellectually and physically accessible, relevant to the visitors' existing knowledge and experience, and that allow for multiple outcomes.[17] School groups may benefit from similarly designed, group-friendly environments.

In attempting to create a holistic model, John Falk and Lynn Dierking suggest that educators consider three contexts: the personal context of how a person learns, prior experience, and motivation; the socio-cultural context that puts learning within the culture and the community in which a visitor moves; and the physical context of the museum surroundings.[18] Lisa Brochu also believes that visitor experience needs to be explained through time and space.[19] She considers five time frames that together define the visitor's experience: the decision-making process to visit, the moment of entry into the museum, the times of connections between the visitor and the museum's messages, the moment of exit from the museum, and a later commitment where the museum experience is turned into a lasting difference in the visitor's life. These models illustrate how important it is to consider more than just the museum lesson in planning for and assessing learning in museum-school programs.

Learning Theory and Museum-School Programs

There are many exemplary instances of instructional practice in traditional schools and museum galleries that museum educators can adapt in designing their own programs, but there also is room for improvement in both. Museum-school partnerships offer a chance to capitalize on and learn from the best teaching practices, and also become laboratories for exploring which theories have the most potential to help all students learn.

As the constructivist learning that began with Dewey and Piaget blossoms in classrooms, formal education has already begun to look like the best of museum gallery teaching. More and more teachers today create cultures and values that address the ways students shape meaning in social groups, use community resources, and place the teacher as learning facilitator. With the current emphasis on making exhibits and programs visitor-centric, museum-school programs also acknowledge the variety of ways in which people learn. Museum educators can create ways for all students, not just some, to learn and voice their ideas through social working groups. This can be done with pair-sharing activities and small study groups in the gallery—groups that write and reflect together, that draw in the galleries and even move kinesthetically in response to objects. These strategies can offer students with different learning preferences a variety of opportunities during the museum visit. In working closely with teachers, museum educators can better understand the prior experiences of students and help to shape the pre- and post-visit experience to sustain learning from the museum experience back in the classroom.

To make museum-school partnership programs as successful as possible, museum educators must make time for theory. Melinda M. Mayer poses a question applicable across museum disciplines. "On what basis, therefore, should (art) museum educators decide the theoretical foundation of their teaching? Once having made that choice, what are the difficulties involved in translating that theory into good practice?"[20] Too often museum educators rush to develop programs and believe they are successful because they see the work resonate with the learner. In fact, these programs may very well be successful, but this information cannot be used to develop future programs unless the learning theory behind the success is considered carefully.

In planning programs, museum educators have an opportunity to stop and consider: What learning theory informs our daily practice? How do we use it as we plan programs? One way to ferret this out is to conduct audits of programs against the basic tenets of multiple theorists.[21] The best program leaves no learner behind—it uses a complement of theories. For example, does the program take into account the cognitive age development of the child *and* does it have elements that reach different intelligences *and* does it consider the various contexts of learning? In reflection, museum educators also may discover and articulate what they are bringing to the theory table out of applied research conducted with student and teacher visitors.

As the future unfolds, crossing the line between strict pedagogical divides in traditional and museum education can only enhance both fields. Researchers from both arenas can work together to create dialogues, conduct research together, make presentations to all types of conferences and continue to enhance each others' efforts for all students.[22]

In the end, all educators, no matter their setting, are looking for ways to create enduring understanding in their students.

NOTES

1. George E. Hein, "The Museum and the Needs of People," International Committee of Museum Educators Conference (1991), http://www.exploratorium.edu/ifi/resources/constructivistlearning.html.

2. S. Bouffard, B. Bridglall, E. Gordon, and H. Weiss, "Reframing Family Involvement in Education" (Research Report, New York: The Campaign for Educational Equity, May 2009). http://www.hfrp.org/family-involvement/publications-resources/reframing-family-involvement-in-education.

3. For an overview of teaching coaching models, see Bruce Joyce and Beverly Showers, "The Evolution of Peer Coaching," reprinted from "The Evolution of Peer Coaching." *Educational Leadership* 53, no. 6 (1996): 12–16 at http://www.sflqi.org.uk/online/materials/02%20Embedding%20SfL/06%20Working%20in%20Partnersip%20(2.6)/06%20Working%20In%20Partnership%20-%20Resource%20Joyce%20and%20Showers%20Article%201.pdf.

4. For an example, see "Teacher Moderation: Collaborative Assessment of Student Work," *The Literacy and Numeracy Secretariat Capacity Building Series,* Special Edition #2, http://www.edu.gov.on.ca/eng/literacynumeracy/inspire/research/Teacher_Moderation.pdf.

5. Arthur L. Costa and Bena Kallick, ed., *Learning and Leading with Habits of Mind: Sixteen Essential Characteristics for Success* (Alexandria, Va.: Association for Supervision and Curriculum Development, 2009) and K.I. Boyess and G. Watts, *Learning and Living with Habits of Mind: The Habits of Mind Learning Tool: Elementary and Secondary Editions* (Alexandria, Va.: Association for Supervision and Curriculum Development, 2009).

6. U.S. Department of Health and Human Services, Administration for Children and Families, "Why Children's Dispositions Should Matter to All Teachers," http://eclkc.ohs.acf.hhs.gov/hslc/ecdh/eecd/Domains%20of%20Child%20Development/Science/WhyChildrensDi.htm, and Andrew Littlejohn, "Digging Deeper: Learner's Disposition and Strategy Use" in *Strategies in Language Learning and Teaching,* ed. G. Cane (Singapore: RELC, 2008), downloaded from www.AndrewLittlejohn.net.

7. See "Education Theory Bookshelf" in the Appendix.

8. We understand that the theory is not as cut and dry as this chapter makes it appear. The theorists have influenced and responded to each other. This chapter, however, emphasizes the major differences in how the theorists approach learning theory as a way to help museum educators think more easily about their own work.

9. Karen Knutson and Kevin Crowley, "Museums as Learning Laboratory: Developing and Using a Practical Theory of Informal Learning," *Hand to Hand,* 18, no. 4 (2005): 4–5.

10. Stephen M. Kosslyn and Oliver Koenig, *Wet Mind: The New Cognitive Neuroscience* (New York: Free Press, 1992).

11. Steven Pinker, *How The Mind Works* (New York: W.W. Norton and Company, Inc., 1997).

12. John Henniger Shuh, "Teaching Yourself to Teach with Objects," in *The Educational Role of the Museum,* 2nd ed., ed. Eilean Hooper-Greenhill (New York: Routledge, 1999), 80-91.

13. Melora McDermott-Lewis in consultation with Patterson Williams, *The Denver Art Museum Interpretive Project, Winter, 1990, http://www.denverartmuseum.org/files/pdf/DAMIntProj_1.pdf.*

14. Tracey Beck, Pauline Eversmann, Rosemary Krill, Edwina Michael, and Beth Twiss-Garrity, "Material Culture as Text: Review and Reform of the Literacy Model for Interpretation," *American Material Culture: The Shape of the Field* (Winterthur, Del.: Winterthur, 1997), 135–176.

15. Karen Knutson and Kevin Crowley, "Museums as Learning Laboratory: Developing and Using a Practical Theory of Informal Learning," *Hand to Hand*, 18, no. 4 (2005): 4-5; and Karen Knutson, "Expertise and Experience: Museums, a Place for Talk,"

http://upclose.lrdc.pitt.edu/publications/pdfs/Knutsonfuture.pdf, July 23, 2009.

16. Paul Gabriel, "Visual Gateways to Memory: How the Brain Makes Visual Sense," (paper presented at the annual meeting of the American Association of Museums, Chicago, IL, May 13–17, 2007).

17. Minda Borun et. al., *Family Learning in Museums: The PISEC Perspective* (Philadelphia: Philadelphia/Camden Informal Science Education Collaborative, The Franklin Institute, 1998).

18. John H Falk and Lynn D. Dierking, *Learning from Museums: Visitor Experiences and the Making of Meaning* (Walnut Creek: AltaMira Press, 2000).

19. Lisa Brochu, *Interpretive Planning, the 5-M Model for Successful Planning Projects* (Fort Collins, CO: The National Association for Interpreters, 2003).

20. Melinda M. Mayer, *Bridging the Theory-Practice Divide in Contemporary Art Museum Education* (Reston, Va.: National Art Educators Association, 2005).

21. See "Planning For A Variety Of Learning Styles" in Appendix.

22. Examples of this movement are historically grounded as illustrated in an article in *Museum News* by Mihaly Csikszentmihalyi & Kim Hermanson, "Intrinsic Motivation in Museums: Why Does One Want to Learn?" *Museum News* (May/June 1995): 35+; and by the AAM *Learning in Museums* seminars that sustain a practice of seeking speakers and establishing conversations with experts from outside the museum realm.

5

Museum Programs for School Audiences: The Basics

Kim Fortney

This chapter seeks to identify and define the essentials of solid, cutting-edge museum programs for schools. It explores and provides examples of each type and delves into the core components of meaningful programs. Strong, well-developed programs are a prerequisite to effective partnerships with schools. Those looking to get started and those looking to reassess will find practical guidance here.

✷ ✷ ✷

There are many kinds of museums and most offer programs for schools. For some museums, these programs are a quaint addition to exhibitions or goodwill gestures to the community. For others, the programs represent the heart and soul of the institution and serve as a direct tool for achieving mission. Some programs generate significant, relied-upon revenue while others are offered free of charge, supported by operations or external funding. Some are directed by professional educators while others are managed by volunteers. Some serve hundreds; others, tens of thousands. The content varies just as widely, ranging from live insects to people of the past. With so much varied programming being offered at so many museums, it may seem unlikely or even impossible to find commonality. Yet good programs share common features regardless of the setting.

Types of Museum Programs for Schools

A museum's cache of offerings to schools features variations on a few standards that are explored here, along with critical components that should be part of each program, regardless of the size or type of museum developing and executing it.

The Museum Experience Formerly Known as the Field Trip

The term "field trip" seems perfectly harmless. It describes what essentially happens: school children take a trip into the field. The problem is that the same term is used to describe a day at an amusement park or a free-for-all in a big city. In this era of accountability to demonstrated relevance, the term no longer fits. The days out of school for pure enjoyment, where maybe learning occurs and maybe it does not, are gone. Students are certainly allowed to have fun, but what they do outside the classroom must relate to curriculum and tested subjects.

Many museum experiences for students have been relevant to classroom learning for decades, although not all have. If museums want teachers and administrators to seriously consider student visits, they must articulate the value of the experience for students in relation to what is being learned at school in addition to its value as an engaging and memory-making break from the routine.

There are options for delivering a museum experience in a way that achieves results. Some work well in certain situations and not well in others. A great example is the Visual Thinking Strategies method. This proven strategy is used frequently in art museums as a means of demonstrating to student (and other) visitors that interpretation is personal, that individual interpretation is valid and that art offers much by merely looking and wondering. It works in other settings as well, but is not appropriate when the museum educator wants students to take away a specific message about something they are seeing.[1] Depending on the content and physical setting of the museum, it may be appropriate to give students prescribed time to view an exhibition or even a single artifact on their own, then bring them together to discuss what they saw and thought about. Another method is the interactive tour with lots of time for questions and answers, which works very well, particularly when the content is challenging or entirely new to the audience. A good museum educator considers the most appropriate strategies for the content, physical setting, time frame, audience size and age.

The hands-on component, sometimes called the studio tour in art museum settings, is a common and important part of the museum experience for students. During this portion, students use skills they already have or learn new ones as they apply concepts they learned just moments ago. Perhaps they are selecting props for their portrait or designing a broadside using printer's blocks. Sometimes these hands-engaged activities can be done affordably so that each child takes a finished piece home. Other times every child adds his/her work to a greater effort that stays at the museum, like a giant patchwork quilt or mural. The making of sensory connections is the point.

Other Add-Ons/Variations

When students visit a museum, there are many things they can do beyond or in addition to seeing an exhibition and engaging in a corresponding hands-on activity. Other options include walking tours of the area around the museum, story telling or reading, and guided play. The museum environment has boundless opportunities for learning. Of course, every program must be developed in accordance with the museum's guiding principles.

Solid Museum Experience Components:

   *development that occurs well in advance, incorporating teacher ideas along with
      those of other museum staff
   *planning that takes place with teacher input before students arrive
   *clear learning goals, tweaked by audience characteristics
   *clearly articulated relevance to curriculum of targeted schools and academic
      standards in every applicable subject area

*sufficient time used well

*enough staff or volunteers so that groups can be divided into fewer than 25 students

*staff or volunteers who are thoroughly trained in a variety of techniques and learning styles, and who are able to adapt on the spot

*a hands-on component that relates directly to the content of the program

*pre-visit stage setting for both teacher and students

*post-visit time for students to process learning

*evaluation at all stages and the readiness to incorporate findings from these processes[2]

After-School Programs

The school day ends around 3:00 pm. Many children need somewhere safe to go until other family members are available. Statistics point to these unscheduled hours as highly dangerous for vulnerable kids. Can museums help? Many have done so by creating programs that run during after-school hours. Some charge a fee to parents. Others are entirely subsidized through government, corporate or private funding. This is not an avenue for museums seeking income-producing programs, as the amount of staff time to develop, manage and nurture these programs can be significant.

At the Newark Museum in New Jersey, Ted Lind, with more than 25 years in the field, directs a model after-school program that is also a well-developed museum and school partnership. Supported through state funding and a small parental fee, the museum created Prime Time 3 to 6 in partnership with a public school district. The program is held in three elementary schools and about 200 elementary-school children attend every day, participating in museum-based activities related to a thematic academic curriculum. The children also benefit from tutoring, healthy outdoor recreation, community service activities and more. The program is licensed by New Jersey as an after-school childcare provider and employs about 21 people. Prime Time 3 to 6 also provides professional development to teachers and special events for parents.

Lind describes it as an incredibly valuable program that is critical to mission but also one that is very labor intensive. Ultimately, though, the museum continues it because of its results, as demonstrated in a statewide evaluation. Lind explains, "Students are doing better in reading and other subjects. The program is providing a safe after-school program and a great benefit to children. Parents and the district love the museum connection, appreciating the value of the museum's staff and collections."[3]

Solid After-School Program Components:

*meticulous curriculum developed in conjunction with many advisers, including teachers, administrators, community leaders and parents

*ample staff in a ratio aligned with state expectations/mandates for childcare providers, and who are screened for direct interaction with children

*a devoted development person who is endlessly seeking support

*sufficient, secure physical space with room to grow

*tested and practiced emergency procedures

*oversight by administrators, youth advocates and attorneys

*continual evaluation with a well-developed mechanism for incorporating results

Presentations in the Classroom

Museum educators offer a variety of curriculum-relevant programs as presentations in the classroom. A museum educator might bring along a few key artifacts or images to make a focused content presentation at a teacher's request; introduce a kit that is borrowed by the class for a few weeks; or arrive in costume, assuming the identity of an historical figure. Sometimes the presentation is the program and offering it enables the museum to explore a content area that is not featured in the museum's exhibitions. Other times the presentation is part of the museum experience, occurring before the students visit the museum.

This type of presentation is practiced by the Walters Art Museum in Baltimore, Maryland. Amanda Kodeck manages the program. Staff members visit schools within a 50-mile radius to deliver a pre-visit lesson that sets the stage for the curriculum-based school tour and studio class that the students will experience when they visit the museum. The classroom visit "helps the kids to feel more comfortable once they come to the museum, particularly if the same person they see at school is the one who leads their studio class at the museum... Having had some exposure to artifacts and images during the pre-visit also increases their comfort level as well as their readiness to build upon recently acquired knowledge."[4]

Solid Classroom Presentation Components:

*developed with audience in mind and with teacher advisers after a survey of
    teachers to determine interest in particular topics

*clearly articulated relevance to academic standards in all applicable areas and to
    curriculum of targeted schools

*timed to the minute to maximize and respect school schedules

*hands-on materials, such as artifact reproductions, image enlargements,
    manipulative activities, clothing, etc.

*learning activities that enable discovery, creativity and individual application of
    content

*a summary of the presentation given to the teacher in advance, to include pre- and
    post-presentation suggestions, and a list of resources for further study

*flexibility to accommodate small and large audiences

*evaluation

Rentable Kits or Trunks

Museums want to be of service to as many schools as possible but recognize that visits to the museum are not always feasible. This is not a new problem. Even in economically favorable times, schools are less likely to travel more than an hour to visit a museum. To address this challenge, museum educators have come up with the concept of a museum visit in a box. These have come a long way over the years, from the rubber tub filled with "mysteries" designed *for* the schools, to carefully planned, content-rich units housed in a container appropriate to the material and designed in partnership with teachers.[5]

Kits have their downsides. While schools that use the kits are being served by the museum, chances are good that schools using them may never actually visit the museum. Another downside is time. While the museum can charge for rental of the kits and the travel expense of staff who visit the school to deliver the kits or present programs related to them, the time that the staff member spends traveling is time away from other projects. Because many kits are rented by schools located a significant distance from the museum, this "lost" time can become burdensome. Staff time is further devoted to the maintenance of the kits, as they must be inventoried and cared for after every use. The Walters Museum offers its trunks to schools beyond a 50-mile radius. Although the program requires staff time to maintain and grow the trunks, Amanda Kodeck believes these resources are worthwhile, especially when serving students who might not be able to experience the museum otherwise.[6]

Solid Kit/Trunk Components:

> *concisely worded purpose
> *clearly articulated relevance to academic standards in all applicable areas and to curriculum of targeted schools
> *clearly articulated relationship between the content and expertise that went into the kit and the other offerings of the museum
> *a guide to using the kit, with multiple suggestions related to time, class size, and subject-area focus
> *durable, hands-on materials, such as artifact reproductions, image enlargements, manipulative activities, etc.
> *learning activities that enable creativity and individual application of content
> *a printed list of resources for the teacher who wants to study more about the content
> *an inventory checklist to be completed when the kit is picked up and returned
> *a durable and easily transportable container that is intrinsic to the content, as opposed to a rubber tub
> *evaluation

Distance Learning Programs

Technology is at the heart of distance learning programs, which are so-named because the audience is physically separated from the teacher but the two can see and hear each other. As with most things technological, when these programs first were developed, the equipment expense was immense and few museums could afford the investment. Those who used it thought it was an amazing tool, as it had the capability of reaching hundreds or even thousands of people at multiple locations with one presenter. A top-notch speaker could lead a program for classrooms around the country without traveling more than a few miles from home.

These programs have come a long way in terms of size, portability, cost and use. In the early days, a museum might only use one to conduct an inferior version of the same exhibit tour that was available to on-site groups. Now the units are portable and wireless, enabling the museum educator and audience to move around and connect with schools that are not hard-wired. The current form requires only a web camera, microphone and webinar software on the museum's end, and a computer lab at the school. John Buchinger, who develops distance-learning programs at the New York State Historical Association, raves about the reach of this technology. "For small museums or institutions that are separated from populations by geography or that must close during winter, this technology offers an exciting, splashy way to reach and build audiences."[7]

Buchinger sees endless interactive capabilities with new webinar platforms. "You can share documents, send objective questions, chat with users, broadcast videos and even send students to specific websites with control in the hands of the program leader." He has seen the positive effects of these programs. "We fill gaps in school curriculum and reach students in a non-traditional way that has real impact on their learning."[8]

Solid Distance Learning Program Components:

   *developed with input of audiences similar to those targeted
   *clearly articulated relevance to academic standards and curriculum of the targeted
     schools
   *a strong marketing effort explaining the hardware/system requirements for users
     and effectiveness of the program
   *interesting content, perhaps utilizing odd items in your institution's collection
   *outside-the-box ideas for interactivity
   *dynamic, vibrant program leaders
   *an advance conversation with the teacher about what to expect
   *resource materials provided to the teacher, including pre- and post-conference
     suggestions
   *evaluation

Incorporation of Model Programs

Museums are great partners with other organizations that offer large-scale, ready-made programs requiring local, regional or state sponsorship. The idea is that an organization with a fully developed opportunity for students joins forces with a museum looking for a nationally-recognized model through which to expand its offerings. Organizations in this category include the Science Fair and National History Day.[9] The museums run the programs in their area using the model of the partner organization. Doors open to schools that are interested in the national program but might be less familiar with the museum. In many cases, teachers who are not as interested in bringing students to the museum might become very active in the national program administered by the museum. This relationship might spill over into awareness and participation in the museum's other offerings.[10]

Sharon Dietz, a teacher who has coached students doing National History Day for 20 years, shares her reasons for using and promoting the program. "Because of the emphasis on primary source research, National History Day is the vehicle that allows teachers to motivate students to move beyond Wikipedia, videos, and their textbooks to discover historical researced . . . After gleaning, evaluating and analyzing information, the students are challenged to synthesize what they learned and communicate it in a creative fashion. Students have produced interesting papers, fascinating exhibits, riveting performances, and exciting documentaries. I've watched these students graduate from high school and go on to college and careers where they continue to use the skills they learned in high school in the National History Day contest."[11]

Solid Model Program Components:

> *clearly defined responsibilities between the museum and the partnering organization
> *carefully articulated relationships between the model program and academic standards and curriculum of targeted schools
> *highlighted resources at the museum and in the community that will help teachers and students who are participating in the model program; these resources are obtained as a result of communication and collaboration with other cultural organizations in the area
> *evaluation.

Putting It Into Practice

Taking Your Programs to Schools

Getting Noticed

Even as recently as 10 years ago, a brochure mailed to schools would start the phones ringing. But in this era, that approach likely will fail. What is needed now is an entirely new way of thinking. Schools will pay attention if they are asked to be included in the development of programs. Engaging teachers and administrators from the beginning will lead to greater interest and better programs. When preparing to market programs, museum educators should help teachers understand how the program will help students make connections, to think critically, to want to learn. Administrators, who will approve or reject the program request, want to see results. They want to know what students will be doing that they cannot do in the classroom and how it will improve test scores. The Newark Museum now holds open houses for administrators as well as for teachers. They devote real time to cultivating relationships with principals and supervisors, facing the challenge head on.[12] Finding ways to connect with administrators is vital to program health.

Soliciting and Developing Partnerships

The following tips for building partnerships with schools are derived from conference sessions at the annual meetings of the Mid-Atlantic Association of Museums and the American Association of Museums. Session attendees contributed to a definition of the ideal museum-school partnership and to this list of tips.[13]

*Do not reproduce the classroom; create an experience that is different from the classroom

*Know the procedures for approval of field trips in targeted schools

*Know the curriculum and how the museum plugs into it

*Develop, state and maintain relevance to standards

*Know the resources (e.g., textbooks) that schools are using

*Develop a mechanism to demonstrate what you will provide and how it augments curriculum

*Know the audience, understand the needs, then look for points of intersection

*Provide resources for teachers and help them connect to those resources

*Prior to a group's visit, structure the program to assess needs of students

*Know both the official and the operative contacts in each school

*Request access to teachers

*Grant authority to the people who are charged with front-line program delivery in the partnership

*Utilize teachers on an advisory committee and get involved in a similar capacity at schools

*Invite teachers to the museum for in-service workshops and structure the experience

*Be clear about the assets of the museum

*Create a safe space for learning

*Evaluate and use the results as evidence of the impact of the experience

*Be organized

*Be flexible; have a plan B

*Offer museum spaces to schools at low or no cost

NOTES

1. To learn more about Visual Thinking Strategies, begin with Abigail Housen's descriptive article, "Eye of the Beholder: Research, Theory and Practice," Visual Understanding in Education (2001). http://www.vtshome.org/system/resources/0000/0006/Eye_of_the_Beholder.pdf.

2. See chapter 9 for detailed descriptions of evaluation processes.

3. Ted Lind, Deputy Director for Education, The Newark Museum, Newark, NJ, conversation with author, 25 November 2009.

4. Amanda Kodeck, Manager, School Programs, Walters Art Museum, Baltimore, MD, conversation with author, 25 November 2009.

5. Examples include those developed by the Heritage Center of Lancaster County, which created *Sunshine and Shadows*, a kit about Amish quilting, in conjunction with elementary teachers and an art specialist, and housed in a easily carried quilted bag. For more information, visit www.lancasterheritage.com.

6. Kodeck, interview.

7. John Buchinger, Associate Director of Education, New York State Historical Association, Cooperstown, NY, conversation with author, 8 December 2009.

8. Ibid.

9. For more information about Science Fair, see http://www.societyforscience.org/Page.aspx?pid=270 and contact science museums that are affiliated with the program. For National History Day, visit www.nhd.org and browse through the map of affiliates. As a point of disclosure, the author is the deputy director of National History Day.

10. Whereas most program types described in this chapter are either most appropriate for elementary- and middle-school students or applicable to all in varying degrees, competitions like Science Fair and National History Day are mostly restricted to middle- and high-school students.

11. Sharon Dietz, Enrichment Facilitator, J. P. McCaskey High School, School District of Lancaster, Lancaster, PA, conversation with author, 23 November 2009.

12. Lind, interview.

13. The Mid-Atlantic Association of Museums met in Pittsburgh in October 2007. The American Association of Museums held its annual meeting in Denver in April 2008. Two hundred people contributed to the tips provided here. Please see "Collective Definition of Ideal Museum-School Partnership" in the Appendix for other outcomes of these conference sessions.

Putting It All Together: A Case Study

Ann Fortescue, Marla Shoemaker, James Stein, and Jean Woodley

The following case study defines the necessary phases of a successful, multi-partner program in Philadelphia, identifying the vital steps from recognizing a school district's need to establishing long-term sustainability. It illustrates much of the guidance of the preceding chapters with a concrete example of a continuing partnership. The tips for "Putting It Into Practice" at the end of the case study provide important guidelines for all such collaborations.

Art Speaks: Connecting Visual Arts and Language Arts

Could a large public art museum with an encyclopedic collection, several smaller partner museums, and a large urban public school district build a long-term partnership? What common need could they address to provide release time for all fourth graders to visit an art museum? The answer to the first question is "Yes," and the answer to the second question is "By reaching out to the school district in a recognized area of need: literacy."

The project came in response to the School District of Philadelphia's (SDP) announcement in 2004 that all students across the district should be given equal educational resources and experiences. With that goal in mind, the Philadelphia Museum of Art (PMA), in partnership with the Barnes Foundation, the Fabric Workshop and Museum, the Institute of Contemporary Art at the University of Pennsylvania, and the Pennsylvania Academy of the Fine Arts, designed a comprehensive program for all fourth graders in the Philadelphia School District, and sought a national leadership grant from the Institute of Museum and Library Services (IMLS) to fund its development and implementation.

The program is Art Speaks, designed to connect the visual arts with language arts. The partnership provides a visit to one of the five art institutions, free of charge, to every fourth grade class in Philadelphia's public schools. Equally important, the visit and all supporting materials align with SDP's core curriculum in both language arts and visual arts, and therefore assist teachers in meeting Pennsylvania's Academic Standards and making adequate yearly progress toward federally mandated No Child Left Behind goals.

Scaling Up the Impact

In order to serve all 13,500 fourth graders, the project was conceived from the outset as a collaboration between five art institutions. The concept was to develop a program in which the content of what was taught was visual art using the five varied collections and exhibitions. The strategies for teaching would be literacy-based, developed from the SDP's fourth-grade curriculum. The PMA spearheaded the strategic conversations among the museum partners to bridge their diverse collections in order to create a single program they could each conduct at their institutions. Their challenge was to carefully craft links with the school district's core curriculum that would meet district learning objectives and satisfy administrators' concerns about releasing students from the classroom to visit an art museum.

Finding Common Ground

A museum team of educators from each art institution met monthly to forge a core experience that they could jointly and individually deliver for students. The partners, wanting to retain each museum's idiosyncrasies while simultaneously finding common ground, planned meetings that alternated between the five sites. This helped each one understand the others' unique strengths and challenges. The Art Speaks team arrived at four questions around which the content would evolve. They also identified fourth-grade literacy skills that arise naturally in discussing art, such as observation, description, interpretation, and expression and support of opinions. Students practiced these open-ended strategies during their museum visit by discussing what they observed, and by writing and drawing in a "Museum Journal," a learning tool used at all the museums. These same content questions and literacy skills were the focus of pre-and post-visit classroom resources.

Asking for Help

An Advisory Committee of fourth-grade teachers, art teachers, SDP administrators in art, literacy, special education and African-American studies, and academics representing art, art education, and literacy met regularly to critique program plans. In addition to offering specific feedback on materials and strategies, committee members proved invaluable in making connections for the team with other decision-makers at the SDP. Several advisors met individually with the writing team to fine-tune the Art Speaks classroom materials so they would seamlessly connect with other SDP fourth-grade learning resources.

Evaluation Became a Marketing Strength

Formative evaluation was central to the development of the program and materials, and also to the subsequent promotion of Art Speaks. Teachers took part in a focus group led by an outside evaluator. Their suggestions were incorporated to make significant changes to the materials and strategies. Extensive testing and ongoing communication strengthened the museum-school relationship and gave the Art Speaks team great confidence in their final product because they had broad-based buy-in from teachers and administrators at the SDP.

Art Speaks formally launched in September, 2008 at a press conference in Philadelphia's City Hall, hosted by the Mayor and the Chairperson of the Philadelphia School Reform Commission (the current governing body for the District). Directors of each museum spoke. There were examples of student work to display around the room[1] and students from participating elementary schools read from compositions inspired by their museum visits.

Sustainability = Fundraising, Promotion and Relevance

Key to city support for Art Speaks is its aim to serve every fourth-grader in public schools, and its promise to offer the program at no cost to the SDP or the city. The original IMLS grant covered costs during initial planning years, and corporate and foundation gifts are now supporting admissions and busing. Devising a strategy for future fundraising remains a challenge. As of this writing, the PMA has committed to raising funds for busing to all sites and for marketing and materials development. Each museum is individually responsible for raising funds to cover admission and other direct costs at that institution.

Throughout the first formal year of Art Speaks, museum partners sought opportunities to promote the program throughout the district, and it is clear that continuing promotion is critical to reaching every student. Strategies have included teacher workshops, meetings with decision-makers, and presentations at meetings of administrators. Because Art Speaks offers new approaches to teaching required literacy skills, it is not hard to sell the program, but getting the word out will continue to take time and resources.

The museum partners continue to meet regularly to strategize these and other long-term issues of sustainability. The ongoing challenge for the Art Speaks team is to adhere to the shared value that the program is successful because it is built to be flexible and able to accommodate change at the SDP, as well as at each institution. The team also recognizes the need to continue to work together to keep the program viable and relevant.

Long-term museum-school partnerships require ongoing work building and maintaining relationships between museum and school district staff on every level—from the museum director and superintendent, curriculum specialists and teachers to those at the museum responsible for education programs. A strong foundation for an effective, responsive partnership that will endure beyond the pilot phase has several key elements. These include a flexible structure, open communication and a shared vision. The flexible structure allows for ownership by each partner, as well as a level of individuality, enabling each partner to do what it does best. Open communication is critical and can save a partnership even when shared vision falters along the way. When all three of these elements are in place, the partnership likely will endure disruptions such as new personnel and will be strengthened by the influx of new ideas.

Putting It Into Practice

Sustaining Museum-School Partnerships

Project Team
1. Clearly identify roles and accountability for team members.

Project Schedule
1. Allow sufficient time in the first year for partners to get to know one another and to develop goals, objectives, and curricula that will work for all institutions.

Allow sufficient time to pilot test materials, and receive input from those whom the project will serve, before final materials are produced (focus group meetings).

Process
1. Keep the project on track.

2. Jointly develop a shared vision that enables buy-in from all partners.

3. Build a flexible schedule and a mechanism for open communication.

4. Rotate location of team meetings among all participating museums so that members come to better understand the institutional culture of each place.

5. Be flexible and open to various approaches to museum education among participating institutions and team members.

6. Be prepared for rough spots when there is no easy way out. Remember that real breakthroughs often occur at key decision points. Alternatively, if agreement cannot be reached around a given topic, then move on to new ideas.

7. Work to ensure that all partners have an equal voice, and all are equally committed to the project.

8. Allow the unique idiosyncrasies of each institution to shine, and find common ground to ensure that classroom teachers' expectations are met at each site.

9. Develop a Memorandum of Understanding to clearly identify each partner's responsibilities to the project and identify financial obligations—both in-kind and funds to be raised for the project. This may take a while to set up, as many schools will need to have their solicitor review and approve it.

Participation and Support by Audience Representatives
1. Create an advisory committee that represents the diverse interests of the partner

schools (including teachers, administrators, and if appropriate, students) as well as other stakeholders at the beginning of the project. Give committee discrete tasks and opportunities for input at key stages of the project.

2. Include this committee, as well as individual teachers, in the pilot phase of the project, followed by focus group meetings.

3. Develop a network of people within the school who can promote the project to teachers and principals.

5. Allow substantial time and resources to raising awareness of and ongoing support for the program in the school, both before and after the project is launched.

5. Make the museum available to the school for activities unrelated to the project. This will bring a wider representation of school employees and stakeholders to the museum where you can share information about the partnership project informally. For example, offer to host a press conference announcing a school-wide achievement, or host a regular principals' meeting.

Funding

1. Identify the funds needed to cover all project expenses: staffing, training, etc.

2. Provide funds to create, test, revise, and produce high-quality, attractive classroom materials.

3. Cover all costs to schools, including buses, for initial years of the project.

4. Plan for future joint fundraising to ensure the longevity of the project.

5. Design the partnership to fit within the current budget of both the museum and the school. For example, the museum could offer to assist in re-writing classroom curricula to coincide with a long-term exhibition and incorporate museum field trips. This has a multi-year obligation that can enable joint fundraising for school and museum general operating and transportation·expenses.

NOTES

1. Art Speaks materials are available online at philamuseum.org/booklets/9_54_109_1.html.

6

Getting Out of the Subject Box

Claudia B. Ocello

WITH CONTRIBUTIONS BY AMY GOICOECHEA, ELLEN PROVENZANO, ELLEN STROJAN
AND COURTNEY WARING

Museum educators need not be constrained by the core disciplines of their institutions. Art museums may be excellent sites for teaching writing skills. Historic houses may yield exciting opportunities to examine architecture, engineering or math skills. Museum artifacts have remarkable potential to link to many topics in the school curriculum. This chapter offers excellent case studies of such cross-disciplinary programs in action and encourages creative approaches to addressing program content.

Picture this: During a fourth-grade museum field trip at the Delaware Art Museum, students from Kuumba Academy Charter School and their tour guide explore how art shares unique stories with the viewer. They look closely at a mixed-media work by Baltimore artist Richard Cleaver, *Queen's Closet,* which focuses on King Henry VIII of England and his six wives, and respond to the work by writing a postcard or letter while they are sitting in front of it. Afterwards they create personal "story-closets" in the museum's art studios. The partnership continues in the classroom where students select a work of art from the museum's website and draft their own unique stories written in the first person from a character depicted in one of the artworks. Some students decide to write as if they were a queen, based on Cleaver's art. An encounter with art becomes a lesson in first person narrative writing.[1]

Picture this: Students from local elementary schools in Glynn County, Georgia are outside, but not for recess. They're uncovering local history by excavating a trench filled with artifacts from the past at Fort Frederica National Monument. After excavating, they go to the archaeology lab at a partner school to clean the objects, research them, and sketch, analyze, and use them to interpret the past. Besides learning local history, they are exploring science, language arts, and math.[2]

And picture this: As part of their science curriculum, second graders in Wyoming read a story about the challenges that winter brings to animals. Then the students visit an art museum—the National Museum of Wildlife Art in Jackson—to view paintings that depict the migratory, adaptive, and hibernation behavior of animals. Students then create their own puppets of Jackson Hole animals and do a writing project based on the artwork they saw in the galleries. Through this program students connect science with art and writing.[3]

What all these programs and many others across the country have in common is how art, history, science, and other disciplines can be integrated across the curriculum in school *and* within the museum. Going beyond the "subject box" that labels museums on the outside can bring school audiences inside the museum and has benefits for all involved. Integrating the content and putting it into a broader context can help teachers explore with students how *all* subjects taught in school can come together and be used to support each other. These connections might even answer the students' question, "Why do I need to learn this?"

Starting these museum-school partnerships requires a meeting of the minds, both literally and figuratively. While teachers and museum educators have a good deal in common, such as an understanding of developmental and learning theory, there may be differences in teaching strategies, goals and objectives, and in understanding curriculum and expectations. The best way to overcome these differences is for classroom teachers and museum educators to get to know each other and start a dialogue on how best to work together.

In some cases, an idea itself becomes the jumping-off point. Kuumba Academy turned to the museum when they realized their limited studio art space was not providing the best art experience for the students. The Delaware Art Museum had the studio space and the contacts with professional artists that the school wanted. Thus, Project ARTSCOPE (Students Creating, Observing, Participating, and Engaging) began as a collaboration to provide a better art experience for the students; it developed into a unique art experience that uses the visual arts to connect with history, language arts, and other content areas.[4]

In 1994, the staff of Fort Frederica National Monument, a unit of the National Park Service that preserves and interprets the ruins of a 1736 British town and fort in Georgia, realized they had their hands full—literally. Park staff discovered a trench filled with over 100,000 artifacts without provenance that had been previously excavated and reburied. Simultaneously, less than a mile away, construction was progressing on a new elementary school. Park staff seized the opportunity to meet with the school principal and administrators to discuss using the trench site and artifacts as educational tools. Archaeology now serves as the theme of the program at the site and exposes students to the many disciplines that come together in the "field" of archaeology.[5]

Other times, it may be best for school and museum partners to meet and brainstorm and let the process develop organically. During three face-to-face meetings, second-grade teachers and museum educators generated shared learning goals to guide the curriculum development process for the program "Wildlife in Winter" at The National Museum of Wildlife Art in Wyoming. Here, museum educators work with teachers to individualize the projects the students complete at the end of their visit. As Amy Goicoechea, associate curator for education at the National Museum of Wildlife Art notes, "Because the program was co-developed, the teachers continue to be excited about using the museum as a resource and about team teaching the curriculum."[6]

Part of the meetings between museum educators and teachers involves museum staff becoming familiar with state core curriculum academic standards. While academic standards differ among states, there is a movement to have states follow national standards.[7] Both museum and classroom educators need to stay current with standards and refer to them at joint meetings. Museum staff also should consider their museum's mission and vision, and any separate education department goals or philosophies. Open communication and shared responsibility to respect and honor these goals, objectives, curriculum standards and guiding principles will form the basis for a successful and meaningful collaboration.

After the collaborative planning stages, museum educators and school staff need to maintain communication to ensure continued success. With Project ARTSCOPE a lead staff member represents each partner organization. While face-to-face meetings may dwindle, emails and phone calls are critical to discuss specific museum lessons, extension activities, and prospective funding possibilities.[8]

This communication should occur internally as well. Museum staff need to communicate with curators and development department staff about the program and its "out of the box" subject connections. Curators can help explore the collections for other connections to the science, math, or history theme, and development staff can look out for new funding sources from non-art or history-related foundations. Classroom teachers can work interdepartmentally with their colleagues in other subjects to encourage them to use examples that will make more connections possible for the students in all related subjects.

Studies have shown that students learn better when learning is connected across disciplines. In their 1989 report, Applebee, Langer, and Mullis noted that while students are learning the facts and content in a given discipline, they are not learning how to think and reason effectively using this knowledge.[9] Interdisciplinary teaching can help provide a context for the students to see how their learning can be carried over to another discipline. Collins, Brown, and Newman argue that as a result of learning being relegated to schools in the 20th century, as opposed to the real-world environment, "skills and knowledge have become abstracted from their uses in the world."[10] Museums can provide the students and classroom teachers with the "real world" situation where they can reason, analyze, and connect their learning across the disciplines and in a context. In turn, when students see the value of what they are learning, they are more motivated and become more actively engaged.[11]

Another reason to get beyond the subject matter of the museum links back to theories of learning and development. Howard Gardner's Theory of Multiple Intelligences[12] suggests that people learn in different ways. Given these differences, it makes sense that teaching across the disciplines might, for example, encourage a learner with more logical-mathematical intelligence to comprehend, appreciate, and become engaged with a painting or historic site when taught through the lens of math or science.

Students engaged in multi-disciplinary partnerships can participate on a more level playing field. One student who participated in the Fort Frederica archaeology program had difficulties with reading and writing, but latched onto the study of archaeology and wrote an exemplary site report for the project.[13] The historic and contemporary photographs and advertisements explored in the National Museum of Wildlife Art's program, "Jackson Hole History: Just Passing Through," is being used by middle- and high-school English Language Learners to both improve their speaking skills and also to help them become more familiar with the history and scenery of their adopted home.[14]

While there are tangible benefits for schools and participants, museums also can gain by expanding their audience through this interdisciplinary approach. Thanks to the National Museum of Wildlife Art's program "There's an Art to Education" (which encompasses the "Wildlife in Winter" program and the "Just Passing Through" program mentioned above), and the strong relationship between the Education Department and the local schools, nearly 75% of all school-aged children in Jackson Hole participate in at least one museum program annually.[15] The Delaware Museum of Art noted that out of approximately 100 students in grades 2–5 surveyed, 46% said they had visited the museum beyond the multiple visit program.[16] Fort Frederica can target and dedicate fewer staff and resources to the partnership program, which frees up other rangers to work on additional tasks.[17] An increased audience of school-aged children and families can lead to increased memberships (both teacher and family memberships), more merchandise sold in the gift shop or spent in the cafeteria, and better use of staff time, resources and museum finances, not to mention the ability to tell potential funders that serving the mission is a high priority in the institution.

Despite all of the successes and benefits, there are certainly obstacles and challenges to overcome in creating these partnerships. Lack of museum staff or volunteers to teach programs sometimes means increasing class size or limiting the number of classes or students per day, per program. Limited funding for school visits will impact the number of programs a museum can offer. Changes in personnel, both in museums and schools, may interrupt the flow of these programs and slow progress. New educators on both sides have to learn the rhythm and steps, and dance through the "red tape" of scheduling and teaching the programs. This change in personnel also may affect the commitment and dedication of staff to the program, and change the dynamics of the partnership. Museums and schools should be aware of these challenges and communicate consistently to help overcome and compensate for them as much as possible.

Changes in education and museum funding have led to increased accountability and changes in priorities to funders of both school and museum programs. With the advent of "No Child Left Behind," teachers' focus turned to improving classroom test scores in math and language arts. This sometimes means less time for field trips, and less time to teach art, history, and other subjects not tested. For museums, this emphasis on testing could mean fewer visits—if your programs are not interdisciplinary. In early spring 2006, a fifth-grade teacher visiting The New Jersey Historical Society for a program on the Industrial Revolution told the museum educator that until now, she hadn't had time to do any social studies with her students because they were preparing for the standardized tests. Her school district let her take the field trip because the museum advertised the program as meeting standards in language arts, which is tested, as well as social studies, which is not tested. Fort Frederica addresses the issue of the focus on test scores by surveying and analyzing student success on targeted, standardized test items that relate directly to the educational goals of their archaeology program. Showing improved student achievement on those standardized test items supports the educational benefits of the program.[18]

Evaluation of these interdisciplinary programs, both formal and informal, is critical to their success. Delaware Art Museum educators show students from Kuumba Academy an image of a work of art prior to their first visit and ask them to respond to it through writing. Upon completion of their four visits, they view the same image again and are asked to respond again in writing. Educators review the writings for more description and details, and 53% of participants included more details after four visits. One third-grade teacher participating in the program noted that "They [the students] are using creative thinking and relating the art to broader issues in history, religion, and things in their lives." Similarly, a docent observed that as students progressed through their four visits, "they participate more, are more focused, and carefully listen to one another." A student nicely summed up his experience saying, "I learned that if you use your imagination, it can get you a lot of places."[19] A teacher working with "There's an Art to Education" program at the National Museum of Wildlife Art explained the program's impact on her students: "Sketching wildlife has always been one of my favorite parts. The way you present this to the children is so awesome and then you let them go and explore. Using the paintings as a model for sketching animals is so great." Anecdotes and numerical percentages are useful for leveraging grant money as well as convincing school administrators of a program's worth.[20]

Educators in schools and museums are both incredibly busy in their own right. It might seem that adding a sustained, interdisciplinary partnership between a school and museum would increase an already overburdened schedule. While there may be extra effort involved, these case studies show that despite many challenges—changing school climates, funding issues, and staff changes—creating and sustaining multi-disciplinary programs benefit museums, schools, and students and may help to sustain programs for both the museum and the school.

Putting It Into Practice

Get to know each other well and extend your teacher contacts to many subject areas.

*Explore and share goals and objectives and mutually respect them through program development and implementation.

*Clearly designate partners' roles at the start of the collaboration.

*Collaboratively develop grade-level programs that are rooted in grade-level standards *across* disciplines.

*Stay on top of trends in education, both locally and nationally.

*Communicate regularly with each other and with other departments in your organization/school.

*Assign a point-person for each partner organization.

*Be flexible!

*Develop and execute an evaluation/feedback plan.

*Offer incentives for teachers and students and their families for continued support of the museum.

NOTES

1. Courtney Waring, electronic communication with author, 3 July 2009.

2. Ellen Provenzano and Ellen Strojan, electronic communication with author, 13 July 2009.

3. Amy Goicoechea, electronic communication with author, 12 June 2009.

4. Waring, electronic communication.

5. Provenzano and Strojan, electronic communications.

6. Goicoechea, electronic communication.

7. M. Glod, "46 States and D.C. to Pursue Common Education Standards." *The Washington Post*, 1 June 2009. Accessed on-line 9/12/09 <http://www.washingtonpost.com/wp-dyn/content/article/2009/05/31/AR2009053102339.html?sid=ST2009060100036.

8. Waring, electronic communication.

9. A.N. Applebee, J.A. Langer, & I.V. Mullis, *Crossroads in American Education: A Summary of Findings* (Princeton, NJ: Educational Testing Service, 1989).

10. A. Collins, J.S. Brown, & S.E. Newman, "Cognitive Apprenticeship: Teaching the Crafts of Reading, Writing, and Mathematics." In L.B. Resnick, ed., *Knowledge, Learning and Instruction: Essays in Honor of Robert Glaser* (Hillsdale, NJ: Lawrence A. Erlbaum Publishers, 1989), 453.

11. L.B. Resnick, "Introduction." In L.B. Resnick, ed., *Knowing, Learning and Instruction: Essays in Honor of Robert Glaser.* (Hillsdale, NJ: Lawrence A. Erlbaum Publishers, 1989), 1–24.

12. See Chapter 4 for more information about the theories of Howard Gardner and others.

13. Provenzano and Strojan, electronic communications.

14. Goicoechea, electronic communication.

15. Ibid.

16. Waring, electronic communication.

17. Provenzano and Strojan, electronic communications.

18. Ibid.

19. Waring, electronic communication.

20. Goicoechea, electronic communication.

Addressing Challenging Topics: A Case Study

Laura Dickstein Thompson

Just as museums have the flexibility and adaptability to address many disciplines, they can also offer supportive environments for discussing sensitive concepts. Through careful planning, they can be trusted and safe environments for encouraging student reflection and discussion about challenging topics. This case study examines two such projects conducted at Kidspace.

Exhibition Projects at Kidspace

Kidspace, a contemporary art gallery, studio, and educational program, promotes the understanding and teaching of art through experiential learning opportunities designed for elementary- and middle-school students, teachers, and families. Housed in the Massachusetts Museum of Contemporary Art (MASS MoCA), Kidspace is a collaborative program founded in 2000 by the Williams College Museum of Art (WCMA), Sterling & Francine Clark Art Institute (The Clark), and MASS MoCA. Kidspace is designed to serve as a partnering mechanism between the three museums and six rural schools in the North Berkshires, and annually provides every student in Pre-K–8th grade with sequential arts education opportunities. The partnership involves teachers, administrators, and three museum staff in the development and assessment of programs. Program elements include: presenting two major contemporary art exhibitions each year; organizing multiple visits to the Kidspace gallery and to the partnering museums; coordinating extensive artist residencies with exhibiting artists; and developing standards-based curriculum with teachers. Kidspace also organizes after-school art classes, family programs, public hours, and website resources.

An important goal of the Kidspace partnership is to present artwork and artistic themes that are not oversimplified just because the exhibitions are intended for children. Kidspace artists are selected for both their works' educational and artistic merit, and are of international and national recognition, such as Long-Bin Chen, Devorah Sperber, and Tim Rollins and K.O.S. By featuring high quality and thought-provoking art, exhibitions promote a belief in children's innate abilities to appreciate, find meaning, and voice opinions and feelings about sophisticated topics. When designing Kidspace exhibitions and educational programming, the Kidspace partnership ensures that a range of materials is explored—for instance, pompoms, pipe cleaners, grass, and found objects—and a range of topics is presented, from childhood fears to wind energy. Contemporary issues like nutrition, war, and the natural environment are brought up through engagements with professional artists and their work, and the partnership uses art as the catalyst for grade-appropriate discussion and activities.

One example of a challenging Kidspace exhibition was *It's Elementary! Empowering Youth Through Art* (October 12, 2006–February 25, 2007), which featured children's artwork from around the world. Five collections of children's art were included: post-World War II paintings from the Columbia University Teachers College Ziegfeld and Angiola Churchill collections; paintings from the New York University Child Study Center created just after the 9/11 attacks; paintings and drawings from the Iraqi Children's Art Exchange Project by Iraqi children living in refugee camps; and prints from the International Child Art Foundation.

Programs included artist residencies, gallery visits with art-making opportunities and an extensive curriculum guide for the classroom. All activities engaged students in discussions that had very personal, reflective, and often difficult elements. For many participants, it marked the first opportunity they had to voice their opinions about what was occurring around the globe and respond to what they encountered in the news media or at home about the wars. While in the gallery, the art inspired children to speak about their feelings concerning the works and their content. They readily got to the core of the work, not only since it was produced entirely by children like them, but because it expressed relatable concepts, like playing with friends or visiting with family. The work also expressed realities that the children were having a hard time grappling with, especially the human faces in the midst of the Iraq war. They were often surprised that the Iraqi children's artwork appeared similar to their own. Some asked why Kidspace had this work on display if "the enemy" produced it? The entire exhibition encouraged students to consider misconceptions they may have had about Iraq and opened them to a discussion that otherwise might not have taken place.

During the school residency with artists, who were graduate students from Columbia Teachers College, elementary students were asked to discuss their personal fears. The students expressed a wide range of fears, from local bullies they may have encountered to global warming, from their parents' anger to sicknesses they have only heard about. Then the students worked in small groups to create wearable sculptures that would protect them from their fears. The combination of this art-making activity with a visit to the gallery, where their sculptures were exhibited, made the experience that much more powerful for the students. Judith M. Burton, professor of art education at Columbia Teachers College, wrote in the exhibition brochure: "Thinking through art makes the world a meaningful place and helps us to know and understand each other… Here we see how the language of art and the shared sensibilities of childhood merge and transcend national boundaries, offering insights into the human dimension of life."[1] The art in the gallery helped to give voice to the concerns the students had about the duality of what should be happy childhood experiences in fearful times.

Kidspace continued to examine this idea of fear in an exhibition titled *It's Rude To Stare* (October 4, 2007–February 24, 2008). The exhibition featured six oversized sculptured figures created by an adult, English-born, Vermont-based artist Richard Criddle. Using wood, bronze, fabricated steel and found objects such as wooden blinds, furniture components and heavy industrial hardware, Criddle brought to life vivid memories of people from his past. Many of the sculptures were inspired by real people who made an enduring impact on the artist, including one of his school teachers who used to slap his wrist with a ruler, a grumpy war veteran who told him stories about being exposed to mustard gas during World War I, and a disabled child about whom his mother told him "it was rude to stare."

Mr. Goodbody (2005), Criddle's depiction of his abusive teacher, stood at almost 10 feet tall and featured scary arms and pointy teeth glaring down at visitors. Elementary school students were invited to sit below the sculpture to take in the full effect of it towering over them. The students were not afraid for the most part, but they spoke about how they could relate to the artist's fear of being dominated by such a powerful and mean person. They showed compassion and empathy for the artist and were delighted that, in a sense, the sculpture had made the ogre look somewhat silly, defusing any power he might have had over children.

When first bringing up the idea of the exhibition, some adults raised concerns about the content, believing that children might be troubled by the experience. As the *Mr. Goodbody* example suggests, the results of the experience were positive and the students were excited about relating their fears to the artist's representations. Criddle believes it was his choice of materials that made the piece seem less threatening and more relatable to children. The lesson to be learned here is that it is possible to tackle difficult topics with students so long as the selection of artwork is comprised of approachable materials.

Considering the Child Learner

Learner outcomes for the two exhibitions were established during the development phase. A year before opening the exhibitions, teachers were asked to consider the potential impact on students and to plan how they could use the art experiences in connection with classroom discussions and activities. Based on discussions with teachers, goals for students were developed, which were used to guide the curation of the exhibitions from selection of works to label content. The goals also became part of the exhibition curriculum guides, and were further explored in teacher workshops where teachers made suggestions for adjustments to programs.

Learner outcomes planned for the two exhibitions focused on students demonstrating an understanding of materials and artistic techniques. Two outcomes targeted the challenging aspects of the exhibitions, whereby students would express empathy for the artists and an appreciation for other points of view. Evidence of empathy and appreciation were voiced in discussions, and also in the form of action. For instance, as part of the *It's Elementary* project, students were asked to send messages to Iraqi children. Students did not hesitate to create elaborate drawings that illustrated positive messages such as peace and unity, which were then sent to Iraqi children living in refugee camps.

The Kidspace learning experiences were rooted in the constructivist theories of John Dewey, presented earlier in this book in Chapter 4. Dewey's belief that both the artist and the beholder go through the processes of selecting, simplifying, clarifying, abridging and condensing through their own interests and perspectives is an important concept in working through difficult topics.

Encouraging questions and providing a safe place for meaningful dialogue are hallmark concepts of the programs at Kidspace. The exhibitions and related programs serve as the instruments through which students interpret what they see and hear from their own perspectives, thus creating their own experiences. Museum educator Lisa C. Roberts states: "Experience refers to new ways of thinking about the basis for knowledge . . . What we know, in other words, is based less on the nature of the object than on the manner and the context in which it is experienced."[2] Museum educators do not design or impose experience on students; rather, they provide the prompts that invite the individual experience to occur and empower students with tools to construct meaning. This pedagogical approach is useful when addressing any topic, whether it is controversial or lighthearted.

The Importance of Trust Among Partners

The vital ingredient in partnerships between schools and museums is trust. This is especially important when addressing sensitive topics in exhibitions and programs. It is necessary for all partners to trust each other to present appropriate materials in ways that are rational and sensitive to the needs, interests, and developmental levels of the children. Teachers and administrators need to buy into and feel part of the formation of the museum's methods to help students feel comfortable expressing themselves verbally and in their artwork. Once a sense of trust has been achieved between schools and museums, the partnership provides the support system to take on these challenges.

Continuity has played a key role in building trust among Kidspace partners. Over 1,000 students from 6 schools are involved annually in programs at Kidspace and at the three museums. Students who were in kindergarten when the gallery first opened in 2000, and are now in eighth grade, have experienced nine years of museum art education, with four museum trips annually (for a total of 36 museum experiences), plus extensive artist residency programs and classroom activities. Because they have an ongoing relationship with museum staff and a clear understanding of the program structure and expectations, the students have come to expect and trust that their thoughts and interpretive reactions will be valued. Evidence of this trust is noted throughout this chapter, when students have demonstrated ease in expressing important details of their lives, and their personal feelings and thoughts. Each year, students are asked to remember past Kidspace experiences, and the ones that seem to stand out in their memories are the exhibitions that challenged them and allowed them to make personal connections to the work.

Curriculum and program development have provided another avenue for developing trust in the Kidspace model. Because Kidspace is deeply rooted in the schools, staff are aware of specific curriculum concerns. For instance, the North Adams schools have been struggling to improve reading and writing test scores. To address this concern, Kidspace organized a meeting with teachers and reading specialists to brainstorm curriculum connections to their reading program. Multi-disciplinary curriculum packets were developed jointly by Kidspace staff and classroom teachers to accompany each exhibition, and priority was given to these materials to connect the arts to the school district's reading textbooks. During the aforementioned Richard Criddle exhibition, Kidspace invited a professional playwright to work with a group of students to write stories about their own childhood fears, and a play based on several pieces in the exhibition. By being in tune with the immediate concerns of the schools, programs and curriculum materials can be tailored to meet their ever-changing needs.

When funds allow, Kidspace has provided stipends for teachers to work on the development of curriculum guides and present them at teacher workshops. These teachers bring new or unsure teachers on board with the Kidspace pedagogy. Moreover, these teachers are useful sounding boards to ensure that ideas for programs and curriculum activities do not go over the heads of the students, or possibly cause negative impact. When dealing with sensitive topics, the teachers readily anticipate most student reactions.

Kidspace was specifically designed by WCMA, The Clark, and MASS MoCA to help support the schools and communities of North Adams and the North Berkshires by creating a safe space for interaction of families, teachers, and students. To that end, the Kidspace founders worked closely with the schools to design a gallery that would engage students with the highest quality art thematically geared toward their interests, and at the same time challenge them to re-examine whatever worldviews they might have. By funding staff, securing grants for everything from buses to art supplies, and making their own institutions accessible to the schools, the partner museums demonstrate to the schools that they are a valued constituency. As a result of this ongoing commitment, the overall partnership has been greatly strengthened.

Putting It Into Practice

Schools and museums that are working together to tackle challenging topics should consider the following recommendations:

*Plan programs that allow for multiple perspectives, are not bound by rigid rules and expectations and are adjustable to the immediate needs of the schools and the student population.

*Think through expected responses to the topic, conduct focus groups to learn more about possible reactions, and be prepared to hear interpretations that might not have been previously considered.

*It is important to design curriculum that encourages dialogue and offers teachers open-ended questions to help them facilitate these activities.

NOTES

1. Judith M. Burton, "More than Meets the Eye: A Look at Children's Art" *It's Elementary!* Kidspace exhibition brochure. North Adams, MA.: Kidspace at MASS MoCA, 2006.

2. Lisa C. Roberts, *From Knowledge to Narrative*. Washington, D.C.: Smithsonian Institution Press, 1997, 132.

7

The Changing Landscape of Museum-Provided Professional Development for Teachers

James Boyer, Kim Fortney, Susy Watts

A true partnership between schools and museums must begin with teachers. Increasingly, museums are offering in-depth professional development opportunities for classroom teachers, providing both methodology and content. These programs assure the seamless connection between formal and informal learning settings, establishing long-term impact for all stakeholders, including students.

꙰ ꙰ ꙰

Seeing the light of recognition and understanding in the eyes of students is a fulfilling reward to the museum educator and teacher alike. Knowing that a teacher has implemented sparks of learning witnessed at museums through museum-led teacher training is far better. A teacher's reach is continuing and has career-long impact. For this reason, museum educators have embarked on the education of teachers in the subject-area content and pedagogical techniques that are the foundation of the museum's offerings for students.

Museums have provided training to teachers for decades, but increasingly, this training includes teachers in the planning, implementation and evaluation of their own learning. This trend mirrors the general movement of museums in the direction of incorporating audience needs, desires and interests into planning and programs,[1] and of schools in varying their pedagogies to reach all student learning styles.[2] With greater frequency, museums are willing to share their authority with the very people they hope to serve. The realm of professional development for teachers is no exception.

Teachers receive innumerable hours of professional development, primarily at their schools, to keep up with changing pedagogies in education. Museums, with their valued collections and human resources, offer the integration of meaningful content with the methods for delivery that teachers know so well. Museums are a living example of the relationship between content and instructional techniques.

Teachers face state requirements for continuing education. While the requirements vary among states, teachers need to accrue scores of hours or units each year. Since the inception of this requirement on a large scale in the 1990s, many states have added conditions, including that all continuing education work fall clearly within the teacher's certification area. Schools in which teachers work have added their interpretations and additional strictures as well. Within this seemingly complex landscape, museums strive to provide meaningful professional development opportunities that teachers want, from which they benefit professionally, and which meet their requirements.[3]

Arts Education Case Studies

In the following section, Susy Watts, an independent museum education professional, offers insights gleaned from research into effective professional development models in arts education. She then presents two case studies, from California and Washington, respectively, which demonstrate these principles.

Museum educators are re-examining the delivery systems they use for training and the focus of their instruction. There is a significant shift to more in-depth training that is process-based over knowledge-focused. Museum educators are training teachers to use museum resources as the highest exemplars of essential understandings[4] that transcend any one example, allowing for applications across cultures and time to the students' present and future—learning and living in the 21st century. Museum educators transfer comprehensible processes to guide students within a museum setting and demonstrate specific strategies to access objects, artifacts, and exhibits in the multiple ways students learn. Training is not limited to a single occasion or even a few days in the summer. Museum educators today are developing informed teaching practices over time and building well-used bridges between the classroom and museum collections/exhibitions.

Museum educators have changed their roles. They leave behind their expert status to develop collaborative and ongoing relationships with teachers within the museum and over time in the classroom. Strong professional development includes the following promising impacts:

*creates clear intentions for training and evaluating intended outcomes;
*develops professional partnerships with teachers in planning, training, and implementation;
*chooses depth over breadth of study using object-based examples;
*models co-teaching with teachers, then coaches teachers in the museum and in the classroom;
*establishes multi-year relationships with teachers;
*seeks teacher autonomy in use of museum resources; and
*capitalizes on community and organizational partnerships for teacher training.

Teacher training is now held to a higher level of accountability than ever before. As accountability levels in the classroom have risen, so museum teacher training models hold themselves responsible for the specific changes they contribute to teachers and their classroom practice. Two case studies from art museums exemplify these changes in professional development:

Los Angeles County Museum of Art (LACMA)—Growing a Philosophy for Teacher Training

LACMA is in its 28th year of professional development programming.[5] Rachel Bernstein,

Senior Education Coordinator, Professional Development for Teachers, has marked and contributed to the changes in professional development at the museum over the last nine years. "In the past we assumed teachers had the natural ability to transfer experiences as adult learners to classroom instruction. We presented scholarly essays and object descriptions; we emphasized an art historical perspective, and shared lesson plans that were long and lacked discussion questions. Today we develop programs that are more relevant to teachers' needs in the classroom, with clear goals and outcomes. Programs are aligned with specific state content standards and we partner with teachers to adapt materials to students' needs. We are focused on providing and modeling strategies for transfer and adaptation to the classroom."[6]

As LACMA looks to the future, they are devoting more time to teacher forums in which teachers address specific topics and the museum provides a dedicated space for teacher exchange of ideas—an intellectual and object-based space. Bernstein continues, "In the Teachers Academy, there is a strong focus on making program content and curriculum more applicable to teachers' work by providing additional instruction that addresses transfer and makes connections. Museums value teachers' skills and their expertise, as well as the contribution they bring to professional development. You just can't hand them a kit. They need practice time to break it down and reflect in learning communities."[7]

Art Museums—In Partnership with a Community Teacher Training Organization

Seattle Art Museum and Tacoma Art Museum collaborate with a nationally recognized teacher-training program, Arts Impact, that strategically addresses the gap between what children need to learn and what teachers know how to teach in the arts. The museum educators capitalize on their collaborative roles in this partnership to extend the work of their museums to a significant number of teachers spread over a large geographic area. Within this mutually beneficial partnership, museum educators work directly as team members with outside professional development staff and regional teaching artists to plan and implement in-depth training over the course of two to four years. The museums benefit from the major federal funding for professional development received by Arts Impact and the embedded organizational structure and services it brings to the partnership. Arts Impact benefits from the deep, object-based expertise of museum educators and the rich resources of the museums. Each organization's resources and expertise are maximized. During a typical teacher training planning meeting, museum educators take the lead in identifying key objects/artifacts from their collections and exhibitions to complement study concepts in response to the developing ideas of professional trainers and school leadership staff. The museum educators actively work with teachers by hosting topical workshops throughout the school year that deepen teacher practice.

Sibyl Barnum, Arts Impact director, says, "The role of the museum educator is integral to the overall professional development program design. They are considered to be a part of the instructional staff. The museum educators' role guides teachers to link classroom instruction in the arts to the exemplar works at the museum so students and teachers see the real life application of the concepts under study. We consistently receive feedback on the power of training in a museum setting. Teachers develop a sense of belonging gained by 'living' at the museum for a week, increasing the likelihood they will use the museum as an ongoing resource."[8] Jennifer Willson, Manager of School, Educator and Interpretive Technology Programs, Seattle Art Museum adds, "Our partnership with Arts Impact reinforces the museum's vision to connect art to life by bringing our most significant resource—our stellar collection of art—to teachers' classrooms and into their students' lives. At SAM we acknowledge educators as professionals at the center of learning, whose significant contributions have the most profound effect on the lives and learning of their students. We feel it is critical that professional development programs build teachers' confidence not only in basic artist instruction, but also in their ability to identify and use art from the diverse cultures and communities of their students. Arts Impact's teacher professional development program builds communities of teachers who are sophisticated in their use of art and culture as interdisciplinary learning tools, and savvy in their use of local community organizations as powerful learning environments."[9]

Science Education Case Study

As good professional development is found in all disciplines, James Boyer, a science museum educator, describes Urban Advantage, a successful partnership between eight New York City science-related museums and cultural institutions and area schools that features core elements of professional development for teachers. The city-funded program trains teachers to become instructors of other teachers and leads to a project for eighth-grade students.

In 2004, The New York Botanical Garden (NYBG) partnered with seven other cultural institutions from New York City (American Museum of Natural History, Brooklyn Botanic Garden, New York Hall of Science, Queens Botanical Garden, Staten Island Zoo, Wildlife Conservation Society–Bronx Zoo, and Wildlife Conservation Society–New York Aquarium) in a program called Urban Advantage (UA). This initiative brought together these science institutions to address the middle-school science Exit Project, which all eighth-grade students in New York City are required to complete. The advantage of the program is that it combines the regional resources and expertise of New York City's institutions to improve science education at the middle-school level. The institutions collaborated to address teacher and student learning, while supplying materials for schools, offering family support, and providing access to the cultural institutions in the form of school and family vouchers.

Because the skills of middle-school teachers are so crucial to the Exit Project's success, the UA Program focused heavily on professional development for first-year participating middle-school teachers, and continued support in subsequent years. The goal of these professional development sessions was to provide teachers with the tools for guiding students through the Exit Project process while using each institution's scientific concentration as a model for doing authentic science. The UA program worked well at providing both content and process skills for these teachers, but early in the second year of the program, the partners realized that a "bridge" was needed to serve as an intermediary between the institutions and the new UA teachers. The partner institutions in the UA Program focus on a wide-range of indoor exhibits, animal habitats, or, in the case of The New York Botanical Garden, outdoor native areas. An understanding of all these environments would be daunting for any professional development instructor, much less a classroom teacher who needs to understand and navigate the many educational idiosyncrasies of his/her classroom, school, and department of education.

To this end, teachers from the first year of the program were invited to become "Lead Teachers," and serve as mentors to new participants. These Lead Teachers brought the first-hand classroom perspective to implementing Exit Projects, generally helped with professional development at each partner institution, provided practical advice and maximized UA opportunities.

In the beginning phase of this partnership, these Lead Teachers were still new to the process of informal science education, as well as its manifestation in these diverse institutions. Through the partnership, the institutions provided in-depth training on how to conduct authentic science investigations, as well as a discussion on how to merge formal and informal science activities. Even though the "learning curve" was steep, this partnership was successful, and the model has continued into the subsequent years of the UA Program, providing new benefits and opportunities to both the teachers and the institutions. After four years of working together, most Lead Teachers are seamless members of the institutions' professional development teams. They carry an equal voice in professional development planning sessions, and bring different perspectives and feedback about activities that are scheduled. They also provide new ideas for conducting middle school science outside the classroom, and these suggestions, in turn, have fine-tuned and expanded the science offerings for students and teachers at these cultural institutions.

In addition, since the Lead Teachers frequently visit these institutions, educating students and teachers, they have become extremely comfortable with how to use the collections, exhibits, and resources of these partners. They have become the strongest advocates for doing authentic science with their students outside of the classroom. Through repeated years of teaching in UA, these teachers have become highly proficient with all aspects of science content taught at their partner institutions. For example, the Lead Teachers associated with NYBG were originally more comfortable with earth science topics, but this multi-year partnership increased their confidence in teaching other concepts, such as plant science and ecology, as well as their mastery of informal education. The confidence and familiarity with these partner institutions comes across as time-tested advice, and this appears to have increased the number of UA teachers conducting offsite science investigations with their students.

Finally, one of the greatest benefits of this partnership is that this opportunity allows the Lead Teachers to share new information and experiences with their students. Their students receive science education from a professional who is adept at science education in the classroom and the field, as well as having the logistical expertise to implement ideas. These teachers understand the advantages of teaching science in New York City, with the availability of many cultural resources, and are able to share their knowledge to improve their students' understanding of science.

Upon entering the sixth year of the UA Program, the dedication of the Lead Teachers cannot be understated, for this "bridge" would never have been built without their commitment. These teachers entered UA with a desire to collaborate with cultural institutions for the experiences that it would bring both personally and professionally, but the key decision to make them equal members of the professional development team made this partnership sustainable. The Lead Teachers bring a different and complementary set of skills and perspectives that are invaluable to effective teacher professional development: the institution as content specialist, the Lead Teacher as implementation specialist. By combining resources in the New York City community, participating UA teachers are given professional development that provides science knowledge (content and process) alongside practical advice for working with their students, which, in the end, translates into students doing authentic science both inside and outside the classroom.

Putting It Into Practice

Museums have many options for providing the professional development opportunities that teachers want and need, from becoming approved by the state to collaborating with approved nearby institutions (including K–12 schools) in the creation of unique partnerships. Whatever your approach in making the opportunities available, here are some tips for success:

1. Find out about your state's requirements for certified teachers and determine if your institution can become an approved provider of hours, units or credits (these terms will vary in definition and usage from state to state).

2. For the target audience, obtain the utilized standards and curricula in the broadest range of content areas that apply to your institution. These documents may be national, state, local or, very likely, a combination. Always consider applicability of content to the language arts curriculum.

3. Talk with teachers with whom you've worked about their experiences with PD. Ask about:

*where they go to fulfill their requirements;
*what resources they utilize; and
*what has transferred well to the classroom.

4. Based upon the outcomes to these conversations and your list of relevant standards and curricula, develop a survey of targeted teachers in your area, asking:

*what the targeted teachers teach, when, for how long, and with what resources;
*how they rate the resources for content that they're currently using;
*to what extent they integrate content across multiple curriculum areas and present it via the pedagogical techniques that they have learned.

5. Using the results of this survey and your review of the other information, consider what your institution can provide to teachers. Investigate:

*the broadest extent of your collections and available resources, including the expertise of staff, stakeholders and members;

*potential collaborations with other institutions (museums, colleges, state agencies, other non-profits, etc.);

*state requirements in terms of hours, frequency, paperwork, etc.

6. Assemble an advisory group of teachers that is representative of your targeted audience to guide the process of developing your programs. Seek the teachers' input and engagement at every turn.

7. Within your targeted audience, find out the time of year when teachers typically plan their PD schedules for the following school year. Begin meeting with your teacher advisors early so that you can incorporate their ideas and feedback into developing programs and be ready to announce during the window of opportunity.

8. Every program has a life cycle. If attendance is dropping after the third year or so, it's time to either revamp or eliminate.

9. Evaluation is particularly critical with PD programs. Through clear learning targets and mixed evaluation methods, you can assess how teachers experienced the session, as well as their retention of content and implementation of new strategies. Conduct these assessments right after each program and at critical points over time, seeking information about how teachers are using what they learned at your PD session in the classroom, which is really the ultimate measure of the success of your program.

Of course, involving teachers in the entire process, from brainstorming through evaluation, will hook them and improve the training itself. If successful, your programs will hold them and word will spread between trusted colleagues and to curious newcomers.

✻ ✻ ✻

NOTES

1. See John Falk and Beverly Sheppard, *Thriving in the Knowledge Age* (Oxford, England: AltaMira Press, 2006) and *Journal of Museum Education* 31, no. 1 (Spring 2006, Museums and Relevancy). A theme throughout the various articles in this volume is the public value of museums as interpreted by visitors.

2. See Arthur L. Costa and Bena Kallick, *Learning and Leading with Habits of Mind: Sixteen Essential Characteristics for Success* (Alexandria, Virginia: Association for Supervision and Curriculum Development, 2009) and Costa and Kallick, *Habits of Mind: A Developmental Series* (Alexandria, Virginia: Association for Supervision and Curriculum Development, 2000).

3. See National Association of State Directors of Teacher Education and Certification (NASDTEC), described fully in the appendix material for this chapter, for state-by-state requirements.

4. See J. McTighe and G. Wiggins, *Understanding by Design* (Alexandria, Virginia: Association for Supervision and Curriculum Development. 1998) and H. Lynn Erickson, *Stirring the Head, Heart and Soul: Redefining Curriculum, Instruction and Concept-Based Learning,* 3rd ed. (Corwin Press, 2007).

5. LACMA Teachers' Academy is an intensive professional development program for K–8 teachers that emphasizes interdisciplinary and practical teaching approaches using works of art in LACMA's collection. Teachers from local schools participate in a five-day summer session at LACMA followed by continuation sessions during the school year. Ongoing evaluation for the program shows the benefits for teachers and students alike and has benefited teachers by contributing to a culture of learning at participating schools. LACMA also hosts Evenings for Educators.

6. Rachel Bernstein, Senior Education Coordinator, Professional Development for Teachers, Los Angeles County Museum of Art, conversation with Susy Watts, June 2009.

7. Ibid.

8. Sibyl Barnum, Arts Impact Director/Director of Arts Education, Puget Sound Educational Service District, Renton, Washington, conversation with Susy Watts, June 2009.

9. Jennifer Willson, Manager of School, Educator and Interpretive Technology Programs, Seattle Art Museum, Seattle, Washington, conversation with Susy Watts, June 2009.

8

Connecting Museum, School and Community: Collaborations for Learning

Julie I. Johnson and Janet L. Rassweiler

Museums and schools are just two of the critical institutions embedded in communities. The art of partnership they have learned together can well be the foundation of programs that combine resources to enhance community life and learning in multiple ways. As illustrated here, these expanded collaborations take the museum further into a meaningful role as a flexible, resource-rich community member, able to serve many audiences in concert with others.

It takes a village to raise a child. —African proverb

Creating opportunities for learning is a significant part of raising a child. Many entities in a community, or village, play a role in this very important task; museums are one. This chapter highlights collaborations[1] that engage students in ways to benefit the community and/or utilize community resources. These projects differ from the traditional museum and school education programs (outreach, kit-based, onsite visits) by capitalizing on the assets in a community, local or regional, to bring richness to learning and deeper connections for students to their surroundings. Whether providing skills development, youth empowerment, or content exploration, the ultimate goal is to develop the best fit between existing resources and school-age audiences' needs.

This chapter provides two types of information: examples of current projects; and considerations for entering multi-organization relationships. Two frameworks important to delivering successful collaborative learning experiences guided the selection of examples for this chapter.

> *The Engagement, Capacity and Continuity Trilogy[2] framework focuses attention on three interdependent factors that must be present in a community for students to be successful. *Engagement* refers to experiences that heighten one's thirst for knowledge and learning. *Capacity* means having the specific knowledge and skills to advance in one's learning. *Continuity* refers to "institutional and programmatic opportunities, material resources and guidance . . .[3]
>
> *The developmental-interaction framework[4] reminds us that children have changing patterns of growth and understanding as they develop and respond to their world. Interaction highlights the importance of engagement with people, materials, and ideas to impact learning.

The ECC framework is helpful in inventorying community assets and identifying potential partners; the developmental-interaction framework should be applied during program development. The examples and discussion are meant to stimulate thinking about possibilities in the community.

Building a Foundation

Historically, museum educators have piloted, assessed, and implemented programs for audiences representing diversity across class, race, gender, and culture, and often have led their institutions to deliver programs that redefine the meaning of accessibility and "non-traditional audiences."[5] Frequently, these programs have been developed with non-museum organizations, many with schools. In order to move into the community more effectively, museums and schools build on existing relationships and skills to create new programs. Each organization contributes unique knowledge about the school-age child, learning theories, and teaching strategies, as well as access to the student's community and the cultural and business community.

What does it take to create vibrant learning experiences that move outside the museum walls and engage community resources? How do you find the right match? As museum professionals have found, and the EEC Trilogy implies, true collaboration requires a significant commitment from all participants. Museum professionals experienced in developing collaborations recommend taking time at the beginning of the relationship to review potential benefits for each organization to inform how all move forward. Possible benefits include:

*increased or new access to expertise and resources
*ability to cultivate relationships
*opportunity to build staff capacity through practice and information access
*exposure to different perspectives and interests in the work of one's institutions
*a mechanism for addressing community concerns.

The strongest collaborations originate from a place where these benefits overlap across organizations, increasing the likelihood of building shared missions.

Working with another organization can be a challenge. Clarity of purpose, process, and outcome are needed; communication is essential. In some instances, partnership may be easier than collaboration. In fact, some very successful collaborations have their roots in early partnership arrangements.

The Oakland Museum of California's (OMCA) *Water Striders Junior Guide Program* is the third incarnation of a program begun in 1993 and initiated as a result of a call from the principal of a nearby elementary school. The principal was concerned about her students going to middle school and being among a more diverse student body than they were used to. Citing teachers' concerns that fifth-grade girls tend to withdraw from active participation in school, the principal believed an OMCA program might help mitigate this situation for her students. The initial pilot was a partnership between the two schools (with different demographics) and OMCA. Students from each fifth-grade came to the museum for training that enabled them to lead tours of the museum for kids from the participating schools.

Fast-forward 15 years: the program has expanded to five schools and now includes a field experience piece in addition to the exhibits training. The program was initially *co-created* with school and museum staff. Each entity contributes resources to the running of the program. Today there is significant energy and synergy between the organizations.

What is needed to go from nascent idea to full-fledged collaboration? According to Barbara Henry, OMCA's Chief Curator of Education, a lot of work went into the growth and evolution of their program. Patience and perseverance are needed in equal measure; building trust is essential. Henry says it is also important that OMCA and its partners co-created the initial goal statements.[6]

Several resources on developing partnerships and collaborations have been published since the original volume of this book. Some are listed in Appendix. While stated differently and often using the terms partnership and collaboration interchangeably, they all have these steps in common:

1. Be clear about mission and goals.

2. Develop a shared vision.

3. Be realistic and question your assumptions.

4. Don't underestimate the need for communication. Communication must exist within and across all organizations.

5. Obtain commitment and support from senior personnel in each organization.

6. Be sensitive to differences in organizational capacity. Sharing resources is important, but one size does not fit all.

7. Review and evaluate.

8. This will take more time than if you worked alone; exercise patience and perseverance: good things take time.

9. Remember, there is no substitute for personal relationships. They can make or break any cross-organization effort.

10. Be flexible, creative and experimental!

Beyond the Walls

When reaching beyond the museum's walls, it is important to remember that while the school day is finite, opportunities for learning are not. Likewise, those organizations with which you might want to build a relationship may have needs that are better met during non-school hours. Schools are seeking alternative ways to engage students and their families. View this as an opportunity for creativity and exploration.

Collaboration ... [entails] learning how to work with the antagonisms, fragmentation, and polarization ....There is a complex interpersonal learning required here that is essential to incorporate [across] various levels of community activity. — Barbara Rogoff, *Cognition, Perception and Language*

Obviously not all schools look the same or operate in the same way. Additionally, programs developed may shift according to needs of the institutions and the broader community.

The Tucson Museum of Art and Historic Block in collaboration with the Tucson Unified School District operate the Museum School for the Visual Arts (MSVA). MSVA had its humble beginnings as ArtWORKS!, an after-school program of the Tucson Pima Arts Council serving students 11–21 years of age. A change in the Council's mission resulted in the program partnering with the Tucson Unified School District and their Department of Alternative Education, becoming the high-school ArtWORKS! Academy. The Academy operated out of a space in a mall for a number of years, with the students actually selling their artwork. When ArtWORKS! Academy lost its space in 2006 the art teacher in the program suggested the program move to the Tucson Museum of Art which had space.

The needs of the Tucson Pima Arts Council shifted as the success of its program grew. Changes in the external environment necessitated changes in the organization and the program. Today, MSVA is the result of a robust collaborative with museum and school district staff co-planning and co-teaching. While the initial move to the art museum was based on space needs, through dialogue and reflection, both organizations came to see a vision and motivation for working together beyond the need for space. Participant feedback has also resulted in varied learning experiences for students as they engage their community. Students actively learn through working with the Alzheimer and Art program for senior citizens or conducting lessons for the general public as part of the local library's book festival.

Focus on Audience

Sometimes a museum has access to resources and expertise that the partner does not; sometimes the reverse is true. In both situations, working together they can develop fuller learning experiences than either could offer alone. For example, a museum may be asked to facilitate programs in support of a particular audience.

The Barringer Infant-Toddler Center sought support from The New Jersey Historical Society to enhance teen parents' parenting skills. Developed in partnership with Barringer, *Partners in Learning: Teens and their Children at Museums* introduces teenage parents to cultural institutions as learning spaces providing opportunities to interact with their children. Over eight sessions, parents and their children visit the Historical Society and other city cultural organizations, try out activities and art materials together, read in the public library, and learn to plan their own trips, recording each experience in a shared scrapbook. As the needs of the young parents change, so must the program, accommodating late afternoon and weekend schedules, travel and school requirements, and childcare needs.

Conversely, a museum may seek to cultivate an audience through a partnership. According to Patricia Sigala, Outreach Educator at Santa Fe's Museum of International Folk

Art (MOIFA), the museum recognized that teenagers were an underserved audience, as many teens had not visited since they came with their elementary school classes. MOIFA enlisted the expertise of Warehouse 21 (W21), a teen art center, to create an event that would establish a relationship between the venues, promote a dialogue between youth and museum, and reinforce the connection between art and music by inviting youth bands to perform at the *Annual Music Night*, now in its 7th year. W21 was integral in connecting the museum with the teenage audience in order to develop a meaningful program with input from teenagers. According to Sigala, "It is important that teens feel they have a place at the museum and that their talents are recognized."[7]

Community Impact

An important reason for connecting with community resources is not only the opportunity for enriched student learning, but also the ability to affect change in the community.

"On March 4-6, 2000, representatives from over 15 marine, estuarine, and natural resource organizations involved in environmental education in Homer, Alaska's Kachemak Bay watershed came together to share their concerns and dreams for science education in their region. They formed an alliance of Kachemak Bay Environmental Educators (KBEEA), envisioning an environmental education system of excellence to inspire life-long learning and commitment to environmental stewardship and sustainability among Kachemak Bay residents and visitors."[8] Members of KBEEA identified the expectations and needs of local and visiting school groups and now provide differentiated experiences and a menu of offerings appropriate for guided and self-guided experiences, ranging from a free *Tidepooling Etiquette* booklet to monthly local Discovery Labs. Members reach into their own organizations to access scholarly expertise and complementary collections for content-rich programs. To help responsibly manage the popular beach site for the future KBEEA is reaching out—to bus companies about group drop-off distribution points and to local community members who work as volunteer tide pool guides.

Environmental educators led these efforts to educate and empower school children and their teachers in service of the world they inhabit. This is an example of the work museum educators are positioned to initiate, support, and sustain as they build programs and relationships with communities outside of their museum's walls. Teaching is "not simply transmitting knowledge and skills; rather . . . working to encourage thoughtful and reflective participation in [a] democratic process."[9]

Sustainability

Building relationships to create and implement meaningful learning experiences takes time and effort. The value these experiences bring to the learner and community is limitless. Their existence and continued presence requires deep thinking and reflection up front and throughout the process. Often sustainability is not considered until the program is running and the kinks have been worked out. In reality though, many of the elements

Sustain: 1) to keep in existence; keep up; maintain or prolong, 2) to provide for the support of . . . . 5) to uphold the validity or justice of . . . —Webster's New World College Dictionary, 4th ed.

that need attention during the initial development of a partnership or collaboration are also important for sustainability. However, one essential question is often overlooked. *What* is to be sustained?

There tends to be an underlying assumption that an entire program must be *sustained*—continued in perpetuity. But is that realistic? Things change at such a rapid pace that keeping a program intact may not serve the best interests of the participants or the organizations involved. The question of what is to be sustained requires planners to be thoughtful about what aspects of a collaboration and program support continued relevance, service and/or growth. Some may choose only for the *relationship* between organizations to be maintained, allowing the initial program to sunset and make room for a future activity. Others may decide that a *program* is so essential to a community that it must remain preserved in its original form. Still others may find during the implementation of the activity that *only a portion* of it works well and should be retained. The possibilities for these outcomes should be explored and made explicit during the initial stages of development.

The desire for program sustainability should not override the need to be relevant and the ability to be flexible. Make the relationships among organizations—museum, school, business, and community entity—the primary focus of sustainability efforts. Preserving this foundation is the key to vibrancy in the current work and possibilities for future efforts.

Determining Success

Similar to sustainability, defining success is a conversation to hold early and often in the development of the program. Chapter 9 of this book discusses evaluation approaches for determining success at the *level of the program*. Here, the focus is at the *level of the partnership*—the multi-organization relationship.

While length of time is one measure of a relationship's success, it does not describe the *nature* of the relationship—the structure, quality, depth of purpose, sense of ownership, development of capacity and the dynamics of sharing. These dimensions give a truer sense of the relationship and will help determine better how and where to make necessary adjustments.

Some factors that contribute to the success of inter-organization relationships include:

*the strength of personal relationships with school personnel and/or community contacts;

*whether and how the project matches capacities of the organizations involved;

*willingness to accommodate each institution's temporary challenges by keeping a project intact and services delivered (e.g., if one partner is experiencing temporary financial challenges, will other partners assume the responsibilities until the crisis has passed?);

*remaining flexible and prepared to revise and adapt the process;
*being intentional about nurturing the relationships.[10]

Incorporating a focus on these factors throughout the life of the partnership or collaboration, as well as steps for building relationships listed earlier, will result in a greater likelihood that conditions will be in place for monitoring progress and gathering evidence of success.

Conclusion

In 2034 museums will be places of cultural exchange in their communities; they won't have any other choice. . . . [Museums] will be one of the most powerful agents in helping all children understand the future . . .[11]

This is a call for museums to increase their role in creating value in their communities. Museum educators should capitalize on the multiple information dissemination systems available to better share successful models, evaluation results and reflections on their process, and practice for effectively building engagement beyond museum walls. Indeed, museum educators could become the collaboration experts in their institutions. They should work inside their institutions to ensure staff understands the value and rationale for working outside the walls.

"The dictionary is the only place that *success* comes before *work*. Hard work is the price we must pay for success. I think you can accomplish anything if you're willing to pay the price." —Vince Lombardi

---

Continuing to build museum-school collaborations that move into the community-at-large will require a change in the museum educator's role and application of different skills for each multi-organization opportunity. The museum's expertise may not be of utmost importance; values rather than content may be the learning goal; and a place to gather together may be more important than time spent in a gallery. At times the need to build on existing knowledge about audiences and how people learn will be necessary. At other times, how to craft meaningful interactive learning experiences or facilitate discussion and reflection will be important. Every opportunity to work across boundaries will be more successful when there is a balance between what the intended community needs and what the museum is best positioned to provide. The ability to respond nimbly will be essential, regardless of the situation. Reach out, explore, experiment and celebrate.

❈ ❈ ❈

NOTES

1. The terms "partnership" and "collaboration" often are used interchangeably. However definitions range from working together toward a common goal (although planning is not shared) to sharing resources in the planning, development, implementation and evaluation of activities in order to achieve a common goal (where the whole is greater than the sum of its parts). For clarity here, we'll use the term "partnership" when referring to the former and "collaboration" for the latter.

2. Eric J. Jolly, Patricia B. Campbell, and Lesley Perlman, *Engagement, Capacity and Continuity: A Trilogy for Student Success* (General Electric, 2004).

3. Jolly, et al., 3.

4. Harriett Cuffaro, Nancy Nager, and Edna K. Shapiro, "The Developmental-Interaction Approach at Bank Street College of Education," *Approaches to Early Childhood Education*, 4th ed. Jaipaul Roopnarine, and James E. Johnson (Upper Saddle River, NJ: Pearson Merrill Prentice Hall, 2005), 8.

5. Mary Ellen Munley and Randy C. Roberts, "Are Museum Educators Still Necessary?" *Journal of Museum Education* 31, no. 1 (Spring 2006, Museums and Relevancy): 29–39.

6. Barbara Henry, Chief Curator of Education, Oakland Museum of California, conversation with authors, 2009.

7. Patricia Sigala, Outreach Educator at Santa Fe's Museum of International Folk Art [MOIFA], conversation with authors, 2009.

8. Kachemak Bay Environmental Education Alliance, http://www.homerfieldtrips.com/id25.html.

9. Nancy Nager and Edna K. Shapiro, *A Progressive Approach to the Education of Teachers: Some Principles from Bank Street College of Education* (New York: Bank Street College of Education, 2007).

10. Benjamin Lorch, Julia Brazas, and Christie Thomas, "Key Success Factors for Museum University-Public School Partnerships" Paper presented at International Cultural Heritage Informatics Meeting (ICHIM), September 8–12, 2003.

11. American Association of Museums, Center for the Future of Museums, *Museums and Society 2034: Trends and Potential Futures* (Washington, D.C.: 2008).

9

Ensuring Program Relevance Through Collaboration and Evaluation

Beth Murphy and Julia Washburn

This chapter explores the role of authentic collaboration and evaluation in all stages of developing and delivering museum programs to ensure that they are relevant to students and a full range of stakeholders, including teachers, school administrators, funders and the museum itself. The authors provide a practical guide for museum educators who are asked to create meaningful connections to their audiences and to plan for, monitor, and enhance a program's resonance using critical issues and learning goals.

※ ※ ※

What's the Point?!

Simply put, if museum education programs aren't relevant, they won't be funded or attended. Program relevance answers the question "What's the point?" for students, but also for teachers, school administrators, donors and the museum itself. The dictionary defines relevance as "relation to the matter at hand; practical and especially social applicability."[1] The extent to which museum education programs are practical, applicable, and relate to the "matter at hand" depends on effective planning, collaboration among stakeholders, and ongoing program evaluation.

The chapter features a partnership between The Bakken Museum and the Minneapolis Public Schools (MPS) serving fourth-grade students and teachers.[2] The program's purpose is to help all students develop a set of strengths—attitudes and competencies which The Bakken calls "Science Assets"—that are indicators of participation, perseverance and achievement in school science, as well as successful workforce participation and civic engagement as scientifically-literate adults. The program goals are accomplished through classroom residencies and teacher professional development linked to the teaching of electricity and magnetism, a core science unit and the content focus of The Bakken. Participating students gain confidence in science, develop creative thinking skills crucial to doing science, discover the role of science in their current and future lives, and become part of a community that values science. At the same time, teachers build their knowledge about science and science teaching skills. They become better prepared to nurture students' Science Assets and foster deeper science knowledge and understanding. The program especially strives to make a difference for students from groups traditionally underrepresented and underserved in science: girls, students of color, and students from low-income communities. Additional museum and school partnerships that have incorporated authentic collaboration and rigorous program evaluation to ensure relevance are highlighted throughout.

The Bakken/MPS School Partnership Program

This program has changed dramatically over its 10-year history. The original program was interesting, unique and undoubtedly focused on the museum's mission, but it was developed solely by museum staff with no substantive input from any external stakeholders. Teachers and students seemed to enjoy the program, but it was difficult to sustain and grow. Real change began to happen when the program manager began asking teachers what it would take to make it work. The Bakken learned that teachers have little time for programs, no matter how good, if they don't address the curriculum and standards for which they are accountable. Later, Bakken staff talked with district science leaders who further emphasized that to be most relevant, partnership programs need to incorporate best practices from formal education, improve student achievement, and promote high-quality teaching. This search for relevance led to big changes, as shown in Figure 1, below.

PARTNERSHIP PROGRAM THEN

One-sided decision making
Input-focused program
Requires extra work from teachers
Most teachers recruited to participate
Minimal district awareness/support
$5-10K in annual grant funding
<100 students per year
Low priority program for museum

PARTNERSHIP PROGRAM NOW

Shared decision making
Outcome-focused program
Supports work teachers already do
Many teachers ask to participate
High district-level involvement
>$150K in annual grant funding
>1,500 students per year
High priority program for museum

Figure 1: *How the Bakken/MPS School Partnership Program changed after focusing on relevance*

None of these changes detracted from The Bakken's mission to "inspire a passion for science and its potential for social good by helping people explore the history and nature of electricity and magnetism."[3] Rather, planning for relevance led seamlessly to discovering a shared vision. Bakken and district staff worked together to refine program goals to address the museum's mission, together with district priorities. The program framework that ensued was something both organizations could support.

In *Franklin Remixed: Ben—The Good, the Bad, and the Ugly*, an online exhibit for middle-school students by middle-school students, four Philadelphia institutions—Benjamin Franklin Tercentenary, Rosenbach Museum and Library, University of the Arts, and Night Kitchen Interactive—joined together to design an inventive educational program using two Franklin-based exhibitions.[4] Authentic collaboration among partners, systematic involvement of students and teachers, and use of evaluation throughout the project culminated in a student-designed online exhibition, which tackles tough issues such as slavery, freedom, and equality in a balanced and provocative context. Beth Twiss Houting, evaluation specialist and co-author of Chapter 4 in this volume, explains that "evaluation helped ensure relevance in a few ways:

1. It helped us to know what the students' knowledge of and attitudes about Franklin were so we did not pitch the curriculum too high or too low.

2. It also allowed us to begin with the students' viewpoint on Franklin (negative and cynical), making the students feel respected.

3. Working with a control group helped us determine the effectiveness of program components in reaching our goals—relevance for future groups."[5]

Giving Everyone a Voice: Achieving Program Relevance Through Collaboration

Collaboration is a "mutually beneficial and well-defined relationship entered into by two or more organizations to achieve common goals."[6] Because the needs and concerns of all stakeholders are taken seriously and addressed in an authentic collaboration, their projects have greater relevance. While many museum educators use collaboration skills on a daily basis, few are aware that there is a body of social science research on effective collaborations that can help deepen and strengthen partnerships. Researchers have identified six categories of success factors that contribute to an effective authentic collaboration:

Environment. A partnership has a better chance of success if members have a history of successful collaboration, the collaborative group is seen as a legitimate community leader, and the partners are working in a favorable political and social climate.

Member characteristics. Important characteristics include mutual respect, understanding, and trust. Partners also see the collaboration in their best interests, and have the ability to compromise.

Process and structure. Partners have a stake in the process as well as the outcome. Every level within the partner organizations is involved, from the executive leadership to the program implementers. Further, the process is flexible, adaptable, appropriately paced and structured. Clear roles and guidelines are specified.

Communication. Partners have open and frequent communication, and establish both formal and informal relationships.

Purpose. Concrete, attainable goals and objectives are established, and partners have a shared vision and unique purpose for collaborating.

Resources. Partners devote sufficient resources to ensure success. Funds, staff, materials, and time are all critical.[7]

The Bakken/MPS School Partnership Program

This theory really does play out in practice. When asked why he thought the School Partnership Program had been successful, Joe Alfano, science curriculum specialist for MPS, highlighted these key reasons: "Program goals benefit both partners, the goals and work are authentic, flexibility . . . ongoing communication, and trust [are built in]."[8] In the School Partnership Program, collaboration happens all the time and at all levels of program planning, implementation and evaluation. Many individuals from The Bakken, MPS and outside organizations have contributed to the success of this program: museum educators and classroom teachers, museum and district leadership, advisors and consultants.

Speaking again on collaboration, Joe Alfano said, "Over and over teachers say, 'This is some of the best staff development I've had.' After hearing this from so many people I realized that they were referring to the synergy of thoughts and efforts, the different perspectives employed and the commitment of all the individuals engaged in this partnership. My relationship with this Bakken partnership has allowed me to see things differently. I now approach organizations that wish to partner with our science department differently. We are in a new era of public education. This partnership we've established represents where we need to be going."[9]

Creating Feedback Loops Through the Tools of Evaluation

Front-End Evaluation

One of the benefits of authentic collaboration in a museum and school partnership is the ease of incorporating evaluation for program development and ongoing feedback. Ideally, evaluation should be a collaborative process and a way of thinking—something the partners do together to systematically design and improve a program.[10] At its best, evaluation is useful to all partners and serves as a catalyst for ongoing feedback and learning. During the program design phase, front-end evaluation can help identify the program's goals and objectives by asking:

*What are the goals and objectives of all partners?
*What are our audience's relevant attitudes?
*What does our audience already know?
*What does our audience want/need to know—what are they seeking?

Front-end evaluation is the start of an ongoing conversation among partners and audience members that will carry on throughout the life of the program.

The Bakken/MPS School Partnership Program

In the fall of 2008, The Bakken began planning for significant program expansion—tripling the number of participating teachers and students in two years. Summative evaluation from the previous two years became front-end research, indicating target areas for improvement. Teacher focus groups identified common themes regarding what teachers liked about the program and their ideas for change. This informed plans for program improvement and field testing. All of this fed the development of the program's "logic model."[11] A logic model is a "systematic and visual way to present and share your understanding of the relationships among the resources you have to operate your program, the activities you plan, and the changes or results you hope to achieve."[12]

Art Speaks! Connecting Visual Arts and Language Arts, a program of the Philadelphia Museum of Art with the Fabric Workshop, the Barnes Foundation, the Pennsylvania Academy of Fine Arts, and Philadelphia Public Schools, created an advisory group with representatives from each partner organization, a curriculum designer and an evaluation specialist. The group used front-end evaluation to ensure that the program was relevant to teachers. One of the lessons learned was that teachers considered themselves literacy experts and felt that the museums should provide fodder for student classroom writing by emphasizing their unique resources and expertise—the visual art, not by introducing writing exercises.[13]

Formative Evaluation

Formative evaluation is used during program development to test ideas, exhibit mock-ups, program tools, and activities. It answers the questions:

*How well does this work?
*How can this be improved?
*Are we missing anything?

This provides another opportunity for stakeholders, especially the audience, to test whether program ideas really work. Of course, the partners must be willing to make changes to improve the program design.

The Bakken/MPS School Partnership Program

Utilization-Focused Evaluation and Backward Design both assume that learning and teaching become more purposeful and meaningful when those responsible for program delivery are deeply involved in establishing and evaluating program outcomes. Because this approach has been used in the Bakken/MPS partnership, teachers more readily understand the program and relate it to other classroom experiences, students make sense of individual program activities in the context of the program as a whole, and museum educators are invested in learning from program evaluation. The Backward Design process builds assessment directly into learning experiences. Thus, at some point in each residency lesson students demonstrate what they've learned, and museum educators modify immediate and future instruction accordingly.

The Rubin Museum of Art's *Thinking Through Art* program is an in-school arts residency that enhances New York City Public School curriculum through arts integration.[14] Evaluation is used to ensure that teachers and museum educators collaborate effectively. The process is supported by the "Evidence of Teacher and Student Learning" template, an online portfolio of student work.[15] The museum educator and teacher use the online material to collect evidence of student learning, communicate with each other, and plan lessons. The online portfolio provides evidence of student learning from class to class, and helps identify where program leaders can modify instruction to meet learning goals.[16]

Summative Evaluation

Summative evaluation is done at the end of a program cycle. It answers:

*What did we achieve?
*What were the outcomes of this program?
*What lessons did we learn?
*What would we keep and what would we change for future programs?

Ideally, partners will use summative evaluation results for developing the next phase of the program, or designing future programs, in addition to reporting results to funders and administrators.

The Bakken/MPS School Partnership Program

Summative evaluation data is collected using mixed methods, such as: knowledge and attitude surveys; informal and formal reflection; interviews and focus groups. For example, student attitude surveys provide information on how the Science Assets of participating students changed during the program. This information is interpreted by different stakeholder groups—museum educators, classroom teachers, museum and district leadership—who summarize findings about the program's successes and challenges, identify program strengths, and make recommendations for future improvements. Involving multiple stakeholder groups enables richer and more complete interpretation. For example, classroom teachers' interpretation was necessary to understand how the program lessons on taking risks and learning from mistakes in science translated to actual behavior changes; students were more resilient when doing science inquiry—trying new things, not being afraid to fail, and learning from mistakes.

Shenandoah National Park, Virginia, offers curriculum-based environmental education programs that enhance classroom instruction through hands-on field experiences.[17] In 2007, Shenandoah participated in a survey project to assess curriculum-based programs in the National Park Service's Northeast Region. The results confirmed that the programs were achieving the intended impact of increasing students' understanding of science content and resource stewardship. They also provided insight into student learning abilities that helped the partners adjust teaching strategies.[18]

Putting It Into Practice

Below are some questions for museum educators wishing to bring greater relevance to new or existing museum and school partnership programs:

1. *Who within the school or district will advocate for the partnership program?* The museum program director should have a counterpart in the district or school to help ensure the program's success.

2. *What local/national trends and standards, school or district priorities, best practices in K–12 education, and other successful programs are important to understand?*

3. *What are the boundaries within which the partnership program must function?* The

program may be constrained by the museum's mission and unique resources, available staff or time, financial limitations or revenue goals, etc. The partnering school or district may also have constraints. Knowing these boundaries in advance will focus the collaboration on what is possible.

4. *What are the unique resources and expertise that each partner brings?* It is especially important to honor the expertise of teachers and find ways to learn from it. Museums should focus on adding to, not replacing, the expertise of teachers. Similarly, museums provide a rich context for learning, as well as creative and engaging approaches to education. Acknowledging expertise facilitates partners learning from each other though capacity-building and formal and informal professional development.

5. *Is the program outcomes-based and is the evaluation utilization-focused?* The specific activities of a program should be designed to achieve program outcomes. Evaluation performed should focus on information that will be useful to all stakeholders for understanding program impact and making program improvements.

Ultimately, program relevance is ensured when program design and evaluation are woven together throughout the entire program cycle and within a framework of ongoing authentic collaboration, as summarized in Figure 2, below.

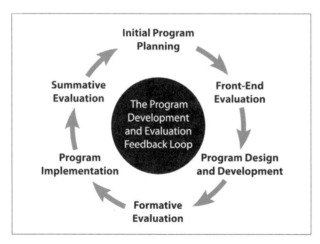

Figure 2: *The Program Development and Evaluation Feedback Loop*

If such a process is embedded into authentic collaboration, program relevance is an inevitable outcome. In short: relevant programs are *created with audiences, not for them.*

NOTES

1. *Merriam Webster's Dictionary*, http://www.merriam-webster.com/dictionary/Relevance (accessed 10 September 2009).

2. The Bakken Museum, http://www.thebakken.org/schoolpartnerships.html (accessed 22 October 2009).

3. The Bakken Museum, http://www.thebakken.org/historyandmission.html (accessed 1 November 2009).

4. Franklin Remixed, http://www.franklinremixed.com/ (accessed 10 September 2009).

5. Beth Twiss Houting, Director of Education, Chester County Historical Society, electronic communication with Beth Murphy, 24 July 2009 and 14 September 2009.

6. Paul W. Mattessich, Marta Murray-Close, Barbara R. Monsey, *Collaboration: What Makes it Work* (Saint Paul, MN: Amherst H. Wilder Foundation, 2001), 4.

7. Ibid, 11-28.

8. Joe Alfano, Science Curriculum Specialist, Minneapolis Public Schools, electronic communication with Beth Murphy, 1 September 2009.

9. Alfano, electronic communication with Beth Murphy.

10. J. Stein, M. Adams and J. Luke, *Thinking Evaluatively: A Practical Guide for Integrating the Visitor Voice* (Nashville, TN: American Association of State and Local History, 2007).

11. See "Logic Model" in the Appendix.

12. W. K. Kellogg Foundation, *Logic Model Development Guide*, 1.

13. Beth Twiss Houting, electronic communication with Beth Murphy.

14. Rubin Museum of Art, http://www.rmanyc.org/pages/load/84#TTA (accessed 22 October 2009).

15. Developed by the New York State Council of the Arts.

16. Marcos Stafne, Head of Education & Visitor Experience, Rubin Museum of Art, electronic communication with Beth Murphy, 29 July 2009.

17. Shenandoah National Park, http://www.nps.gov/shen/forteachers/curriculum-based.htm (accessed 22 October 2009).

18. Tim Taglauer, Education Specialist, Shenandoah National Park, electronic communication with Beth Murphy, 17 August 2009.

10

Paying For It

Betsy Bowers, Jennifer Michaelree Squire, Mary Jane Taylor

The previous chapters have articulated the importance and impact of quality museum and school partnerships. They have identified creative strategies to build relevance, connect to multiple subject topics, and build strong, complementary and curriculum-related programs. While few would argue with the value of such programs, a critical question remains: who will pay for them? This chapter details the financial questions at the heart of preserving museum and school partnerships and examines a variety of useful funding strategies.

In recent years, school field trips to museums have increasingly come to seem like a quaint tradition of the past. Sustained state and local budget challenges threaten to eliminate any "frills," and school field trips, sadly, often fall into that category. Volatile fuel prices have led to sometimes-exorbitant bus fees, making the per-child cost for even a local field trip out of reach for many schools. At the same time, museums are wrestling with wrenching economic decisions. Institutional resources are stretched thin by shrinking investment portfolios. Earned income is reduced and support from cash-strapped individual, corporate and foundation donors is in decline. How can museums address their own financial challenges, reach out to school audiences, fulfill their missions, and keep a balanced budget?

Museums and schools both face a basic financial question: How can they accomplish their goals while spending within their means? Programs for schools are one potential revenue source for museums, and identifying the financial role of school programs is part of a larger discussion about institutional financial stability. This chapter presents viewpoints from multiple perspectives on the subject of school program costs. Feedback about school program fees was solicited from three key groups of stakeholders. The views of those museum executive directors, classroom teachers, and museum educators from across the United States inform this chapter.

To Charge or Not to Charge?

How museums determine school program fees is complex and varied. Approximately a third of the museum educators surveyed said that their museum charges a fee all of the time, while about a third of the staff said their institution always offers programs for free. The remaining one-third of museums sometimes charge a fee, most often depending upon the program or service requested by the school. Admission in many of these museums is free for teachers, chaperones, and students, but a docent-led tour or a hands-on class is available for an additional charge. Some museums charge admission to schools based upon geography; museums have forged relationships with local government and school leaders that allow schools within the city or county limits to bring students to the museum for free. In other instances, special funding allows museums to waive fees for a certain offering or a certain time frame. Some institutions can be flexible about their fees based upon a school's ability to pay, waiving the admission for any school that meets certain economic criteria. In these situations, a teacher often provides proof of eligibility when registering for the museum program.

When museums do need to charge fees, scholarship funds are one way to help maintain broad access to school programs. Such funds are typically raised from individual donors, foundations, government grants and corporate support, although some museums include these costs in their annual budgets. The funds commonly cover bus costs and student and chaperone admission fees. Scholarship funds are offered by just over half (55%) of the museums in our sample, with a school's Title 1 status being the most frequently-cited qualifying criteria.[1] The percentage of students receiving free or reduced price lunch is another oft-used determining factor for awarding scholarship monies. Most museums ask classroom teachers seeking the funds to apply through a formal process, with monies being awarded on a first-come, first-served basis to eligible groups. A few institutions wisely allow teachers whose school does not qualify under the scholarship guidelines to apply for scholarship funds for individual students in their class who cannot pay the admission fee. This farsighted and compassionate view costs museums little, but helps guarantee that kids facing tough times at home are not left out of an important class learning opportunity.

Waiving fees for schools can bring museums increased problems with last-minute cancellations or no-show schools. Such instances often result in direct monetary losses to the museum, with part-time staff needing to be paid for their scheduled time. But there are also "opportunity costs" every time a school does not come for a program they reserved, as the museum could have offered the time slot to another school group, or used the classroom or gallery space for other, perhaps income-generating, purposes. Some museums have successfully addressed this challenge with such policies as charging teachers a nominal refundable fee or placing a hold on a school credit card.

Sharing the Costs

When choosing to visit a museum, classroom teachers carefully evaluate many factors. They look at the ease and cost of transportation, the suitability of scheduling options, the likelihood of the visit being a fun trip for students, and how well the program connects to state and national standards. But two concerns are paramount: the content of the program and the trip's cost per child. Teachers must carefully weigh the cost per child, the cost per chaperone, and the cost of transportation to determine if the trip is feasible. These are the trip costs (along with fees for food) that teachers, students and families often must find a way to fund.

As the chart below summarizes, both museum educators and classroom teachers report that schools use a combination of resources to pay for their visits to museums. Costs often are shared between annual school budgets, students and parents, the partnering museum, a community foundation or corporate sponsor, and parent-teacher organizations. It is important for museum directors and educators to realize, however, that the ultimate financial burden for field trips falls squarely on the shoulders of classroom teachers. It is they who often lead class fundraising efforts to subsidize expenses.

Who Usually Pays	Adminitrations/ School Districts	Student or Parent	Classroom Teacher	Partnering Museum	Community Foundations or Corporate Funding
Top Costs Covered	Substitute Teacher	Admission Fees Lunch/Snack	Materials	Admission Fees Transportation	Admission Fees Transportation
Other Costs Covered	Transportation Admission Fees Materials Lunch/Snack	Transportation	Chaperone Fee	Lunch/Snack Materials/ Resource	Materials Lunch/Snack

Leadership Perspectives

Museum directors make many difficult decisions about what types of programs and partnerships to pursue. When it comes to paying for education programs, the return on investment (cost compared to long-term benefit) can be nebulous. In this sample, museum executive directors overwhelmingly recognized that partnerships with schools support the museum's mission and believed that such partnerships should and would be continued, even if the program was not revenue-positive. In voicing their approval of such partnerships, the directors identified many less tangible benefits, recognizing that the museums' work with schools provides positive public relations and builds strong community ties. Partnerships with schools also allow museums to pilot programs, receive feedback from partnering teachers, and can lead to the creation of other programs. Working with the school audience also may lead to new museum volunteers, attract the support of local officials, as well as identify ways to work with and strengthen collaborations with other community organizations and museums.

Significantly, directors cited that partnerships matter because potential funders are attracted to strong community relationships. Some even noted that their museums are required to partner with schools to receive certain types of funding. Museum educators, however, cannot become complacent about promoting the overarching importance of school programs to the museum's success. It is critical for educators to seek opportunities to articulate the significance of their work to museum stakeholders and decision makers.

It is also essential for educators to help the museum leadership understand that it is rare for a museum's school programs to be a profitable enterprise. Generally, school programs lose money for an institution, or at best barely cover their costs. Surveyed museum educators reported that public and family programs, especially summer camps and birthday parties, frequently subsidize school programs.

Mission, Budgets and the Bottom Line

In corporate America, success is defined by the bottom line. The black and white indicators attached to positive and negative cash flow determine whether a company should continue on its current course. Non-profit organizations have to consider less tangible factors in determining their direction. As Jim Collins points out in *Good to Great and the Social Sectors*, "the critical question is not 'How much money do we make per dollar of invested capital?' but 'How do we deliver on our mission and make a distinctive impact, relative to our response?'"[2] To help determine the answer, Stephen Weil presented a success/failure matrix for museums in his January/February 2005 AAM *Museum News* article. He provided four specific parameters for museum professionals to consider in determining success: purpose, resources, effectiveness, and efficiency.[3] Articulating purpose is second nature to many museum educators. Determining the resources required for a program or partnership to achieve its intended purpose is much more difficult. A program's effectiveness is determined by whether the intended program purpose is achieved. In the broadest of terms, programs that successfully influence new understanding, interest, attitudes, behaviors or skills in the participants can be considered effective. Running programs efficiently is as important to the success of the institution as effectiveness. Efficiency is indicated when resources used to implement a program remain on or under budget, achieve intended outcomes and meet goals related to the number of participants. A carefully constructed budget is an important first step in determining whether a program should be pursued.

Budget for Success

Preparing a thoughtful budget and presenting it to museum decision makers or program funders is critical to building a strong museum-school partnership. The budget provides an important opportunity to outline the resources involved to implement the project, and to tie their efficient and effective use to long-term results. Budgets also provide a chance to communicate the significance of the program. Although creating practical budgets is a time-consuming process, it is a critical exercise to determine whether the initial partnership should be pursued and whether it should continue in subsequent years. For planning purposes, this budget may be incorporated into the organization's overall budget or presented as a project budget to a potential funder. Below are the key costs that should be included in the financial plan.

*Staff time—Budgets should reflect the percentage of time salaried employees will spend on creating content, building the relationship, and implementing and evaluating the program. In addition, employee benefits should be factored in at about 20% of the salaries. Costs for any contract personnel needed to create curriculum or implement activities also should be included.

*Museum overhead—These expenses are significant and can include individual line items for office rent, utilities, insurance, and administrative costs. Or indirect costs can be lumped together and calculated at about 25% of the program budget.

*Visit costs—Monies may be needed for food, student and chaperone admission, teacher workshop expenses and student transportation.

*Staff travel—Staff driving back and forth to the school should be reimbursed at the federal mileage rate.

*Program materials—Funds should be allotted for designing and producing any printed materials, and buying, cleaning, repairing and replacing any teaching items.

The most significant resource is staff time. Building meaningful and lasting partnerships takes time—a lot of it. Before convincing museum leadership that a museum-school partnership is important to pursue, a thorough and realistic look at the intended population being served should be completed. It is at-risk students in public schools that many, though certainly not all, significant partnerships attempt to serve. Ironically, the complex administrative infrastructure within those school systems can set the stage for a difficult partnership. As museums identify potential school partners, they would be wise to determine how invested and motivated staff and students are in the partnership's success. Notice response time and follow-through on the part of the school staff. If calls are not returned and e-mails not answered, museum educators likely will find that on-going communication will be labor-intensive, and the partnership difficult to keep on track.

Once a school-museum partnership is established, it is difficult to end, even if the program is gravely inefficient and, ultimately, ineffective. The museum educator can be swayed by the relationships built with students; when working directly with the children, the museum's efforts seem immediately worthwhile. In determining how to best use limited resources, though, museum directors may conclude that it is not a good business decision for the museum to continue exerting resources to a project that has a limited impact.

Measuring effectiveness is critical to the success of museum-school partnerships, as evaluation increases the ability of museum and classroom educators to articulate the value of their work. While measuring program outcomes remains a challenge for museum educators, they must provide evidence that a partnership has benefited students and helped the museum move closer to achieving its mission. Whether using external evaluators or in-house staff, museum educators should prepare evaluation tools to provide evidence that they have had an impact on their audience.

In such evaluations of school-museum programs, museums should strive to collect both quantitative and qualitative data. Numbers-based evidence might include traditional summative surveys of teachers and students, but it might also take the form of observational studies in which skilled data collectors watch student behavior, and record the students' levels of engagement. For individual and foundation donors, qualitative evaluation can be equally important. Museums should encourage teachers to assign students to write and draw about their museum experiences, as those student responses and products can be gold mines of information about what students enjoy, value and learn from museum programs. To give these age-old tactics a 21st-century twist, museums can explore creating areas on their websites for students to comment on their experiences.[4]

As museums and schools struggle to find ways to continue valued and effective partnerships, they have the opportunity to re-think what kinds of student contact can sustain learning and build strong relationships. While many educators consider the ideal partnership to be one where the students make frequent visits to the museum to see collections and interact with staff, museums can explore how they can utilize classroom visits and video-conferencing to reduce costs without impairing student learning. Technology in the museum, the classroom, or as homework may help build connections while reducing costs and attracting funders. Creating a blog that shares students' learning, utilizing social media to make connections with the museum and program, or creating a wiki that links the activities at the museum with the classroom are just some of the ways that technology can play a role in museum and school collaborations.[5]

Ultimately, how museums pay for school programs is a measure of a non-profit organization's responsibility to the public. Does accountability to the general population require that museums provide free or low-cost access to the highest quality programming for school children, despite the significant costs of these programs? Or should the museum forego such expensive initiatives, instead opting for less costly programs that contribute to the institution's bottom line, and ensure its survival? It is the hope of the authors that museum directors, educators and classroom teachers will continue the lively debate around these issues at the very heart of the museum's mission.

Putting It Into Practice

As the museum educator determines whether or not to charge for a program, the following guidelines will help.

> *Know what you want and need, and why.
> *Clearly articulate your rationalization with museum leadership, funders, and potential partners.
> *A good plan will take you far.
> *Take the time to plan the program and all connecting aspects (logistics, marketing, etc.).
> *Details matter.
> *Develop a detailed budget that anticipates all costs.
> *Communication is critical.
> *Include those involved in the partnership in the planning and execution (school administration, teacher advisory board, parents, funders, etc.).

*Allow the program room to grow.

*Conduct informal and formal evaluations during program development and once the program is established.

*Give yourself a cushion.

*Recognize that it may take longer and cost more than expected.

※ ※ ※

NOTES

1. Title 1 is a program sponsored by the U.S. Department of Education that provides supplemental funding to local school districts to meet the needs of at-risk and low-income students.

2. Jim Collins, *Good to Great and the Social Sectors* (New York: HarperCollins Publishers, 2005).

3. Stephen E. Weil, "A Success/Failure Matrix for Museums" *Museum News* (January/February 2005): 36–40.

4. See chapter 9 for more information about evaluation.

5. The National Building Museum's Outreach programs demonstrate that the use of technology can be affordable. By using Facebook and a blog to share progress, share activities, post pictures, as well as make important announcements, the students remain connected to the program, staff, and each other. Students without Internet access can work with museum staff who will post their submissions on the blog. NBM also has computers available for the students during the programs. Visit http://iwwl.blogspot.com/.

11

The New York City Museum School:
The Ultimate Museum-School Partnership

Ronald Chaluisan and Sonnet Takahisa

The authors of this chapter provide a reflective history of their experience developing and managing the New York City Museum School (NYCMS). This is an historical document that describes the remarkable achievements of a collaboration that resulted in an altogether new and boldly developed learning entity: The New York City Museum School.

> "Our fondest memory was the colonial history module. Our son played Abigail Adams in a conversation with Phyllis Wheatley and George Washington about slavery. He understood that this issue set the stage for the Civil War and the Civil Rights movement in a way that couldn't have been communicated through a textbook. Being able to interact with primary sources and scholars in our great museums was a remarkable experience." —NYCMS Parent

Overview

The premise of NYCMS is that museums provide opportunities for engagement, exploration, discovery and the creation of knowledge; museum collections provide the foundation for an academically rigorous education. But should museums take on the responsibility of educating children? Specifically, why do so in a 6th–12th grade environment? Unlike other collaborative "projects" between museums and schools, we created an institution with unique structures and new jobs that could not be abandoned upon the completion of funding. And we had to reconcile the expectations and accountability measures in the very different worlds of formal and informal learning.

We were appointed co-directors of the school. Sonnet Takahisa had 20 years of museum experience and Ronald Chaluisan was a master teacher. Bringing complementary experiences to the partnership, for nine years we were jointly responsible for all aspects of the school: hiring, curriculum and professional development, assessment, supervision and administration. Each year, we were equally accountable for 400 6th–12th grade students. Through our personal collaboration, we brought our professional worlds together to provide a model for the NYCMS community and to establish a school in which students used museum resources to meet all city and state curricular mandates. The first group of high school students graduated in June 2001.

Institutional and Administrative Commitments

In 1992, Community School District 2 of the NYC public schools (CSD2) and partner museums (American Museum of Natural History, Brooklyn Museum, Children's Museum of Manhattan, The Jewish Museum, and later New-York Historical Society and South Street Seaport Museum) were awarded a grant to establish a small, community-based school. After two planning years, The New York City Museum School (NYCMS) opened as a middle school that grew annually until all 6–12th grades were established.

The entire NYCMS community was part of imagining a "museum school." Staff, students and parents knew what to expect from a "museum" and understood the concept of "school." But a museum school was original.

Funding was of constant concern. At quarterly meetings, CSD2, museum representatives and school staff discussed budgets, funding, and public relations. NYCMS students and staff regularly presented at museum board meetings, press conferences, VIP events, and teacher workshops.

In 2002–2003, two years after the first high-school graduation, the school's budget was $2.5 million. Two million dollars (80%) came from tax-levy dollars based on per pupil allotment and reimbursable state and federal funds, covering classroom teachers, a co-director/principal, and mandated support services. In addition, CSD2 reimbursed the Brooklyn Museum for the salary of the second co-director. The remaining $0.5 million (20%) represented museum allocations for dedicated educators and interns, ranging from half-time to full-time equivalent positions, reserved museum facilities and supplies.

Development departments at CSD2 and the museums worked together to solicit grants; approximately $225,000 of the museums' expenses was supported by new resources and $275,000 was underwritten by general operating support and grants for educational activities.

All NYCMS faculty, including museum staff, benefited from CSD2's significant commitment to professional development initiatives in literacy and mathematics teaching, lesson and unit planning, and analysis of quantitative and performance-based student assessments.

How do you create an institution that is "in-between" two traditions?

We began NYCMS with the following design principles:

Museums and traditional classrooms are used equally as active learning environments; access to collections of scientific specimens, works of art, historical documents, and artifacts give students opportunities to understand how traditions of knowledge are constructed.

> *Instruction combines the academic rigor of a college preparatory school with the engagement of an elementary school.

*Regardless of academic history, all students meet or exceed state graduation requirements.
*Learning activities are modeled on the practices of museum professionals.
*Collaboration and shared responsibility are mandatory.
*Learning assessments include traditional and progressive standards-based strategies.

We created structures, explored concepts and content mandates, developed expectations for colleagues and students, established agreements, and invented systems and rituals for the school. We studied our students' progress, reflected on these principles, redefined our roles and responsibilities and honed our practices as professionals who journeyed between the formal and informal learning worlds.

In determining that students would spend significant amounts of time in museums, one external concern was: "When will they get their real work done?" Others were concerned about turning open-ended explorations in museums into "school-like" experiences. We grappled with a variety of questions: What is an appropriate scope and sequence for the school? What do teachers and museum educators need to know and be able to do? What should students do in the galleries, and in their classrooms? What is the relationship between these experiences? Is the overall experience coherent for students? Are some teaching strategies more effective in museums and others more effective in classrooms? How should student learning be assessed?

Structure

Students reported to the NYCMS school site. They attended 45- or 90-minute core classes. To maximize time in galleries and minimize loss of instructional time to travel, we block-programmed: middle-school students spent almost two full days, and high-school students spent at least two afternoons in the museums.

During that time, every 8–10 week cycle, students worked with a classroom teacher and a dedicated museum educator on a project that developed observational, oral, written, mathematical, scientific, creative, and technological skills. Students processed data collected at museums and integrated it with information from core classes. Students presented their new knowledge to peers, faculty, families and museum experts. Through this course of study, students were prepared to meet city and state requirements.

The Museum Learning Process

In the beginning, NYCMS teachers, museum professionals and students explored museums and studied objects to support content learning. Despite enhanced resources and focusing on effective co-teaching in the galleries, classroom practice did not change. Faculty and students struggled to reconcile the different expectations of museum and classroom learning.

In the fourth year, we codified The Museum Learning Process™ (MLP™)[1] by articulating the habits of learning that support the construction of knowledge based on primary sources: extended observation, questioning, research, analysis and synthesis, presentation, and reflection. Echoing the learning practiced by museum professionals, students would learn to observe objects for longer periods of time and over time; develop questions and seek additional information from a range of resources including other museum collections, textbooks, literature, the Internet, and subject specialists; analyze and synthesize information to construct their knowledge; share what they learn with peers and the public through written, oral and visual presentations; accept feedback, consider strengths and weaknesses of their presentation; and develop next steps.

The explicit articulation of these habits was an important turning point in the history of NYCMS and has had the most powerful impact on our respective growth as professional educators in museum and school reform.

We mandated that faculty use MLP™ in all aspects of their teaching: discussing a mathematical problem, designing a scientific experiment, studying a map, or reading difficult text. For example, the "Museum Learning Process and Math"[2] asks students to itemize what they see in the problem of the week, prompts them to ask questions, research, gather additional data, identify patterns or rules, present their step-by-step solution, and reflect upon their process. In this way, students are given ample opportunity to practice and master MLP™ in classrooms and in galleries, building their ability and confidence to confront and solve problems everywhere.

We added mastery of MLP™ as a goal for graduation and began to develop indicators for each of the six components. To qualify for graduation, NYCMS students had to revisit and enhance individual projects from subject-based classes and museum modules to provide evidence of their progress in mastering MLP™.

Professional Development Activities

Staff came to the school trained to teach in either classrooms or museums and brought diverse experience to content and knowledge of student development. As we created new instructional structures, we designed professional development experiences to challenge the status quo. All members of the NYCMS community were expected to consciously learn from one another. Museum educators had to know subject area scope and sequences; classroom teachers were expected to teach in museums. All were expected to use a variety of strategies to assess student learning. Without much introduction, relative strangers were expected to teach together and share equal responsibility for student learning.

"Forced collaboration" ensured that teachers and museum educators taught together and learned to work differently. Staff-led workshops enabled professionals from different worlds to experience and incorporate new strategies for curriculum development, teaching and assessment of student learning. The schedule also allowed for co-planning, retreats, and group and individual meetings with school administrators, staff developers, and museum curators.

> Most importantly, students learn to slow down and look. A difficult piece of text, confusing chart or detailed map reveals more information when they literally looked at it longer. —NYCMS History Teacher

Staff workshops were held in museum galleries. At the core of all professional development activities was the notion that looking carefully and systematically describing objects uncovered knowledge, biases, connections and questions. The "Object Observation"[3] protocol developed by Brooklyn Museum educators encourages longer and closer looking skills that lead to increased articulation and interpretation skills, and stimulate curiosity and research. Object Observation encourages educators to use listening as a teaching tool, and helps them recognize diverse perspectives, interests, concerns and skills among students.

Classroom teachers and museum educators attended all CSD2 professional development activities. The common language, structures and learning behaviors in MLP¨, coupled with CSD2 approaches to literacy and mathematics instruction provided coherence to teacher and student practice at NYCMS. The distinct classroom and museum environments provided complementary opportunities to practice various strategies for identifying students' strengths and needs; together teachers and museum educators developed an academic program that encouraged all students to effectively demonstrate their learning.

Curriculum-based Museum Modules

Teaching teams imagined, designed and implemented new modules of interdisciplinary study that gave the museums and classrooms equal status. They articulated common learning goals, allotted the use of time during module study, coordinated instructional activities in museums with those in classrooms, and determined the evidence of learning required from students' final projects and other assessments.

These 8–10 week modules, developmentally-appropriate and geared to curricular mandates, allowed students to explore required content while mastering literacy, mathematical and MLP¨ skills. NYCMS staff designed and continued to refine 28 distinct 6–12th grade museum modules. Middle-school students completed four interdisciplinary modules each year, including studies of Egypt, Life Sciences, Colonial America, Oceans, Geometric Animations and the Amazon. To align with required New York State Regents examinations, the high-school module projects included Evolution, World Religions, the Renaissance, Chemistry and Conservation, Human Rights and Seeing New York.

Surrounded by authentic resources, students wrote and sketched for observation, did academic content research, integrated information from a variety of sources and experimented with different strategies to demonstrate what they learned. Students benefited from behind-the-scenes work with a cross-section of professionals and from examples of high quality presentation, including written materials, visual exhibitions, and public programs. Students wrote object labels for new audiences, created exhibition proposals, planned and implemented programs, and engaged family and the public through exhibition tours. Students were trained to recognize criteria for excellence and moved toward these professional standards in their own work through ongoing assessment and reflection.

Our NYCMS student progress report reflected the "blended" learning goals; class-room teachers and museum educators contributed equally to these quarterly assessments.

In the "Colonial Portraits" module, seventh-graders studied American paintings and decorative arts at the Brooklyn Museum to understand concepts of power and wealth, researched biographies and historical records of American Patriots, created portraits based on art historical traditions, and developed written and oral presentations through which they related the stories of individuals. Finally, they imagined the "conversation" that might occur by juxtaposing unlikely portraits in a gallery.

After several years of success on state-wide humanities assessments, high-school teachers focused on improving student outcomes in Biology. They redoubled efforts to incorporate the American Museum of Natural History as the focus for the study of Evolution. Students observed the similarities and differences of animals within a species and developed hypotheses to explain how variations might have occurred. They studied Darwin, and used his research as the basis for dramatic presentations to explain the theory of evolution and conflicting views of both historical and contemporary scientists.

When 50% more students passed the required examination, teachers developed module projects on the chemical aspects of preservation of works of art with conservators at the Brooklyn Museum, and on the physics of buoyancy and travel through water that determine naval architecture and shipping routes with staff at the South Street Seaport Museum.

> An [alumna] said, "I really miss module" ... (S)he explained that she learned so much ... because of what she did (drawing and writing observations and going different places) and how the teaching was different from the rest of her learning experiences ... The museums allowed for learning that complemented what was taught in classrooms and provided real-world learning experiences.
> —NYCMS Museum Educator

Implications and Lessons Learned

While most discussions of museum learning focus on the behaviors of visitors, we wanted curators, historians, scientists, educators, and designers to model the learning inherent in their work with primary resources. We wanted students to have similar experiences—and to learn by slowing down and revisiting objects over time.

NYCMS became a "learning laboratory" for educators and museum professionals to plan collaboratively, develop museum-based learning modules and observe and document how students and educators learn in and from museums. The unprecedented access to and use of the museums' collections supported adolescents of diverse racial, ethnic, economic, and academic backgrounds in a participatory learning process. Our students were comfortable sharing their knowledge in any museum gallery with the many NYCMS visitors.

NYCMS educators consistently used CSD2's balanced literacy methods in subject areas and museum module classes. Strategies for improving literacy were also built into the MLP¨; students described in detail, compared and contrasted, took notes, hypothesized, re-read, asked questions, and reflected on their learning.

Although our tenure at NYCMS pre-dated No Child Left Behind, we were part of CSD2 where student performance was monitored and meticulously studied. From 1999–2001, we saw gains in middle-school students' English Language Arts scores and high passage rates on the high-school Biology (Living Environment), Global Studies, American History and English Language Arts exams. While we saw gains in these literacy-based classes, we struggled to help teachers and students meet the same benchmarks in mathematics.

In June 2002 all students in our second class of high-school graduates were accepted to 2- and 4-year colleges, many with significant scholarships.

Fifteen years after opening, NYCMS continues to do well, although there have been changes. In 2006, CSD2 phased out the middle school and doubled the number of high-school students. The current administration has expanded its relationships with museums, and students go to museums every Friday afternoon. The school is popular, receiving 10 applications for every seat. For the last three years the school has received an "A" on the city's School Progress Report and a "Proficient" on its Quality Review.

NOTES

    1. See "Museum Learning Process" in Appendix.

    2. See "Museum Learning Process in Math" in Appendix.

    3. See "Object Observation" in Appendix.

Museum Schools: Brief Descriptions and Roster

Keni Sturgeon

Over several decades, a handful of school districts and nearby museums joined to create an innovative educational organization that blends formal and informal learning: the museum school. Museum schools may be defined as "... a school that is collaboratively designed and implemented through a partnership between a school district and at least one museum in order to implement 'museum learning',[1] with at least one of the following three application activities: object creation, exhibit creation, and museum creation."[2] Museum schools offer focused, experiential learning aimed at helping students acquire higher-level thinking and critical analysis skills.

※ ※ ※

To date, museum schools, many of which are magnet schools (public schools that offer specialized courses or curricula), are situated within public school districts. Their funds per student, teacher-to-student ratios, and student demographics are on par with other schools in their district. The main difference is that museum schools have partnered with one or more community institutions—museums, galleries, zoos, botanical gardens, etc., to support the school's learning goals. The relationship that is forged is mutually beneficial to all—school, museum, teacher, and student. The partnerships generally involve a high degree of interdependence among the collaborating institutions.

At museum schools, the mandated curriculum is incorporated into museum-related themes or units. The students and teachers may use objects and exhibits at museums as primary and secondary sources, learning and performing research, analysis and synthesis throughout the curriculum.

The list below is a roster of known museum schools in the U.S., with URLs (when known), grades served, dates of establishment, brief descriptions, and affiliated institutions/organizations.

Museum Schools in the U.S., organized alphabetically by state

Arizona

Flagstaff Arts and Leadership Academy, Flagstaff
http://www.fala.apscc.k12.az.us/
Grades Served: 9 through 12
Established: 1996

The Academy's goals include making learning relevant through the integration of disciplines, concepts, and methodologies, and developing an appreciation of the arts in the lives of its students. Museum Partner: Museum of Northern Arizona

California

Arroyo Seco Museum Science Magnet School, Los Angeles

http://www.arroyosecomagnet.org/
Grades Served: Kindergarten through 8
Established: 1972; became a "Museum Science Magnet" school in the 1990s.
This school is committed to giving students academic preparation, with a museum science focus, providing real-world connections to abstract concepts learned in the classroom.
Museum Partners: Kidspace, Los Angeles County Museum of Art, Audubon Center at Debs Park, Autry National Center, and the Natural History Museum of Los Angeles County

Science Center School, California Science Center, Los Angeles

http://www.californiasciencecenter.org/Education/ScienceCenterSchool/ScienceCenterSchool.php
Grades Served: Kindergarten through 5
Established: 2004
This is a neighborhood school for underserved children and their parents, and is the result of more than a decade of collaborative work between the California Science Center and the Los Angeles Unified School District (LAUSD). Students learn through active participation in an enriched curriculum focused on science, mathematics and the use of technology.
Museum Partner: California Science Center

The Museum School, San Diego

http://museumschool.sandi.net/
Grades Served: Kindergarten through 6
Established: 1998
The Museum School's mission is to celebrate, nurture and enhance the abilities of participants through experiential, project-oriented applied learning, using the wealth of resources in San Diego.
Museum Partners: Originally chartered and run by the *San Diego* Children's *Museum through 2007.*
Today, partners include the San Diego Aerospace Museum, Museum of Photographic Arts, San Diego Museum of Natural History, the Museum of Man, and the San Diego Zoo.

Zoo Magnet Center, Los Angeles

http://www.zoomagnet.net/
Grades Served: 9 through 12
Established: 1981
The Zoo Magnet Center is a small high school of the North Hollywood High School, offering students a challenging college preparatory curriculum focused on animal studies and biological sciences.
Museum Partners: The Los Angeles Zoo and Botanical Gardens, the Autry National Center, and the Natural History Museum of Los Angeles

District of Columbia

Robert Brent Museum Magnet Elementary School

http://www.k12.dc.us/schools/brent/
Grades Served: Kindergarten through 5
Established: 1996

Museum-focused curriculum and instructional practices incorporate a variety of learning activities to meet the educational needs of diverse learners, enabling them to explore, explain and exhibit.
Museum Partners: The museums of the Smithsonian Institution

Stuart-Hobson Middle School
http://www.capitolhillclusterschool.org/
Grades Served: 5 through 8
Established: 1996
This school's program combines traditional classroom work with the study of primary sources, drawn from the vast collections of the country's largest and most diverse collection of art, history, and science resources. Students prepare their own elaborate exhibitions in which they demonstrate what they have learned.
Museum Partners: The museums of the Smithsonian Institution

Florida

Miami Springs Middle School, Miami Springs
http://www.miamisci.org/msms/index.html
Grades Served: 6 through 8
Established: unknown
The staff and community of Miami Springs Middle School exhibit high academic aspirations for all students through a school atmosphere based on harmony, motivation and a desire for excellence, as students develop skills and enhance their self-esteem.
Museum Partner: Miami Science Museum

Shenandoah Middle School Museums Magnet, Miami
http://shenandoahmiddle.dadeschools.net/
Grades Served: 6 through 8
Established: 2005
The Museums Magnet program at Shenandoah Middle School combines the resources and collections of Miami-Dade's museums and cultural institutions to create innovative, multidisciplinary educational experiences for students.
Museum Partners: Dade Heritage Trust Program, Historical Museum of Southern Florida, Lowe Art Museum-University of Miami, Miami Art Museum, and the Wolfsonian-FIU

Southside Elementary Museums Magnet School, Miami
http://southside.dadeschools.net/
Grades Served: Pre-K through 3
Established: date of transition into a museum magnet school unknown.
A humanities-based curriculum, infused with museum resources and expeditions, provides hands-on, minds-on authentic learning experiences taking students beyond the walls of the classroom.
Museum Partners: Miami Art Museum, Historical Museum of Southern Florida, Lowe Art Museum, Miami Museum of Science, Dade Heritage Trust, Vizcaya, and the Wolfsonian Museum

Illinois

Talcott Fine Arts and Museum Academy, Chicago
http://www.cgnaweb.org/Talcott.html
Grades Served: Pre-K through 8
Established: 2005
Talcott strives to provide students with engaging standards-based academics in a safe and nurturing learning environment.

Museum Partners: Art Institute of Chicago, Field Museum, Mexican Fine Arts Center Museum, and the Chicago Children's Museum

Massachusetts

Elias Brookings Expeditionary Learning Museum Magnet School, Springfield
http://www.sps.springfield.ma.us/schoolsites/brookings/default.asp
Grades Served: Kindergarten through 8
Established: date of transition into a museum magnet school unknown.
Staff and students work on projects that help transform the school into a living museum. Students learn through rigorous academic content and service to the community.
Museum Partners: The Springfield Museums – Michele & Donald D'Amour Museum of Fine Arts, George Walter Vincent Smith Art Museum, Springfield Science Museum, and the Connecticut Valley Historical Museum

Fitchburg Museum School, Fitchburg
http://www.fitchburgartmuseum.org/
Grades Served: 5 through 8
Established: 1995
All academic subjects are taught in galleries using an arts-integrated, collections-based curriculum. The school's educational needs drive curatorial decisions concerning the Museum's exhibitions and collections.
Museum Partner: Fitchburg Art Museum

Michigan

Henry Ford Academy, Dearborn
http://www.hfacademy.org/
Grades Served: 9 through 12
Established: 1997
The Henry Ford Academy provides a rigorous, relevant, and unique educational experience to a diverse student body.
Museum Partner: The Henry Ford Museum

Minnesota

Museum Magnet School, St. Paul
http://museum.spps.org/home.html
Grades Served: Pre-K through 6
Established: unknown
Students focus on exploring, researching, creating, and presenting museum quality exhibits to share their knowledge with other students, families, staff, and community members.
Museum Partners: The original partnership with the Science Museum of Minnesota broadened to include other museums.

School for Environmental Studies ("Zoo School"), Apple Valley
http://www.district196.org/ses/
Grades Served: 10 through 12
Established: 1994
The School is a unique partnership between Independent School District 196, the City of Apple Valley, and the State of Minnesota (Minnesota Zoo). Using an interdisciplinary thematic curriculum,

students are involved in projects at the Zoo and in the community.
Museum Partner: The Minnesota Zoo

New York

Dr. Charles R. Drew Science Magnet School, Buffalo
http://www.buffaloschools.org/DrewScienceMagnet90.cfm
Grades Served: Pre-K through 1
Established: circa 1980
Developmentally appropriate educational experiences enable students to achieve the literacy and
numeracy expectations of the New York State Standards.
Museum Partners: Buffalo Museum of Science and the Buffalo Zoo

Genesee Community Charter School at the Rochester Museum & Science Center, Rochester
http://www.gccschool.org/
Grades Served: Kindergarten through 6
Established: 2001
This local history-based and globally-connected program immerses children in investigation and
discovery, extensively using the cultural and natural resources of the community.
Museum Partner: The Rochester Museum & Science Center

Museum School 25, Yonkers
http://ps25.ypschools.org/home.aspx
Grades Served: Pre-K through 5
Established: unknown
The curriculum is enriched as students use artifacts and artwork found at museums that are
related to their instruction in social studies, science and English.
Museum Partners: The Hudson River Museum and others

The New York City Museum School, New York City
http://www.nycmuseumschool.net
Grades Served: 7 through 12
Established: 1995
The New York City Museum School integrates the city's museum collections of scholastic and
artistic assets into established curricula to engage students in authentic learning experiences, while
meeting New York State Board of Regents standards.
Museum Partners: American Museum of Natural History, Brooklyn Museum of Art, South Street
Seaport Museum, and the Children's Museum of Manhattan

North Carolina

Brooks Museums Magnet Elementary School, Raleigh
http://brookses.wcpss.net/news.htm
Grades Served: Kindergarten through 5
Established: 2002
The Brooks School incorporates Howard Gardner's multiple intelligences, along with Paideia
strategies and museum explorations, to allow students to gain information about what they are
studying.
Museum Partners: North Carolina Museum of Science, North Carolina Museum of Art, North
Carolina Museum of History, Marbles Museum, and the Durham Museum of Life and Science

Moore Square Museums Magnet Middle School, Raleigh
http://www.mooresquarems.wcpss.net/
Grades Served: 6 through 8
Established: 2002
This interactive learning environment expands beyond the classroom walls to the museums, the community and the world to prepare students for future success. Dynamic partnerships with local and state museums, government organizations, performing arts centers and area businesses offer students a springboard to knowledge.
Museum Partners: African American Cultural Complex, Artspace, Contemporary Art Museum, Joel Lane House, North Carolina Capitol Building, North Carolina Legislative Building, North Carolina Museum of Art, North Carolina Museum of History, North Carolina Museum of Natural Science, the Pope House, and the Raleigh City Museum

Tennessee

Normal Park Museum Magnet School, Chattanooga
http://www.normalparkmuseummagnet.com/
Grades Served: Kindergarten through 8
Established: 2002
This school seeks to instill lifelong intellectual curiosity, sound judgment and deep understanding by building a solid foundation based on meaningful exploration and discovery through collaborative partnerships with parents, museums and the community.
Museum Partners: Creative Discovery Museum, Hunter Museum of American Art, Chattanooga African-American Museum, Chattanooga Regional History Museum, Chattanooga Nature Center, Tennessee Aquarium, and the Chattanooga Zoo

Texas

Fort Worth Museum School, Fort Worth
http://www.fwmuseum.org/mus_school/
Grades Served: Pre-K & Kindergarten
Established: 1949
For 60 years the Museum School has been opening young minds to a world of natural wonder, combining natural and physical sciences, history and anthropology with art, music and literature, to provide age-appropriate learning experiences that enrich children's lives.
Museum Partner: Fort Worth Museum of Science and History

NOTES

1. S. Takahisa and R. Chaluisan, "New York City Museum School" (paper presented at the Museum School Symposium: Beginning the Conversation, Barcelona, Spain, 1995).

2. Kira S. King, "Alternative Educational Systems: A Multi-Case Study in Museum Schools" (PhD diss., Indiana University, 1998), iv.

A Closing Reflection

Beverly Sheppard

I was 10 years old when I first saw Picasso's *La Vie* in a museum. I stood before it for a long time. I ran my eyes along the sinuous curving lines, over and over. I looked at the empty space between the couple and the woman with the baby. I didn't know what it meant, but it felt so lonely. I was transfixed by the solemn tones and the absolute stillness of the scene. I finally tore myself away and ran to find my sister, taking her by the hand to share this remarkable painting with me.

I know today how lucky I was to spend my Saturdays in a museum. For years I took classes at the Cleveland Museum of Art and made many discoveries among the collections. My self-directed learning wasn't particularly scholarly, but it offered me whole new ways to see the world. My sister and I selected our own "objects of the week" to share with one another. Though few moved me as La Vie did, they all became components of my world in a deeply personal way.

I am reminded of those experiences as I read through the contributions to this book, each filled with the desire to bring museums into the lives of students. Here is a wealth of the most essential practical and pedagogical advice. Each author has brought a passion and conviction about the importance of museums working with schools. Each has designed and implemented remarkable programs that support standards, build curriculum connections, and marry the formal to the informal in complementary ways. The book is filled with tips and advice and examples of what works, and it offers a wonderful bibliography of references for even more information. I am amazed at the talent and insight of so many people committed to every child's learning. To so much wisdom, I add one last thought.

Many children will visit a museum for the first time on their school outings. They may never come again, but even that single visit may encompass a singular and stunning encounter. The careful work we are doing in building partnerships always carries the potential for such a life-changing experience. As we have seen in the many thoughtful ideas within this book, museums have so much to bring to a child's deepening understanding of the world. They can build relationships with otherwise abstract concepts found in their school texts and present the "real thing" that can be seen nowhere else. Just as we want our school visitors to learn, we want them to be filled with wonder at a world that reveals strange new things, that fuels curiosity, and invites them to explore images and ideas that move them beyond the familiar. We want them to feel welcome and empowered in this place called a museum, and to use their own questions to look more deeply and perhaps more critically.

When we build school and museum partnerships, we open the possibility of a personal connection. Such moments are something we cannot orchestrate, but we can provide the setting and the structure where they may take place. Perhaps one last piece of advice as we make our careful plans is to leave a little "free" time in the school visit schedule. Make sure that there is space for a few precious, unstructured moments for students to wander and explore a personal interest. Our goal will remain the same: to merge the school and museum experience for its ultimate impact. We will do so committed to making certain that the unique quality of each partner is well used, that the museum can still be experienced as the magical place it is.

I will always believe that education is the voice of the museum, the framework that distinguishes our most important work. But I also will encourage us all not to confuse learning with schooling or education with memorization. When the museum sets the stage for the visitor's discovery, it creates the inspiration to learn. It evokes new understandings and expands a child's awareness of his or her personal world. Both are at the heart of a learning partnership.

Even before that year when I set off to explore the galleries in Cleveland, I had decided that I wanted to be an artist. When I stood in front of *La Vie*, however, I understood that desire more fully. Somehow I began to realize that art went much deeper than a replicated image—that an artist took on a greater responsibility in revealing the world. In a few quiet moments in a welcoming museum I experienced just the slightest shift in my understanding, just enough to understand how learning in a museum can transform a child's life.

Appendix of Useful Materials

Many of the contributing authors to *An Alliance of Spirit: Museum and School Partnerships* have provided useful materials, such as references, templates, and guidelines for your use. With one exception, the Appendix presents them in the same order as the chapters themselves.

Collective Definition of Ideal Museum-School Partnership

An early step in the process of revisiting museum and school partnerships more than a dozen years after the publication of the original *Building Museum and School Partnerships* was to identify and describe what a partnership between these two venerable institutions looks like in the 21st century. Professionals in the field contributed to a growing definition of the ideal museum and school partnership at the annual meetings of the Mid-Atlantic Association of Museums in October 2007 and of the American Association of Museums in May 2008. A total of 200 people participated in both sessions and offered the following to this multifaceted collective definition.

Characteristics —The ideal partnership:

*features clearly articulated realistic expectations from both parties
*features mutual trust—particularly that follow-through will occur as promised
*provides for mutually adopted goals
*allows for disclosure of other partnerships
*provides full disclosure about what each party can and is willing to provide
*has mutual buy-in at the level of teacher and museum program leader
*solves problems together
*provides for mutual flexibility
*has shared goals and missions
*has quality education as the mutual goal and benchmark
*reflects needs and resources of both parties
*has the right players at the table/all levels of school officials and museum reps
*conducts evaluation/feedback, leading to modifications as needed
*has adequate funding (sustainability, accessibility, capacity)

*contains options for all parties

*provides for equal effort

*contains support from administration on both sides

*has a plan for succession

*provides for a relationship that is under constant review and revision

*reaches people outside the school experience

*demonstrates where curriculum is applicable to the real world

*does something special that can't be done anywhere else

*is a rich relationship that grows

Benefits for both parties—The ideal partnership:

*enables communication

*fosters development of a sense of mutual empowerment

*has applicability to multiple age groups/age-appropriateness

*is generally sustainable/able to be replicated and adapted

*overcomes the challenges associated with transportation costs in bringing students to the museum and vice versa

*overcomes the challenges resulting from No Child Left Behind

Benefits for museums—The ideal partnership:

*creates lifelong museum goers

*results in increased visitorship

*allows museum educators to be in charge on site but respectful of the role of the classroom teachers

Benefits for schools/teachers—The ideal partnership:

*matches needs of schools with resources of museum

*provides resources for teachers

*eases teacher stress

*helps teachers meet Annual Yearly Progress

*helps teachers with cross-curricular ideas

*allows teachers to develop their own trips

*creates museum-driven curriculum development

*enables museum-driven curriculum implementation

*provides content expertise not available in school

*meets state standards

Benefits for students—The ideal partnership:

*is fun!

*creates meaningful and inspiring experiences

*provides students with choices

*helps students get excited about learning

*places student/learner experience at the center

*accommodates multiple learning styles

*results in love of and curiosity about subject

*introduces students to inspiring, passionate professionals as role models

*fosters future career awareness

Planning For A Variety Of Learning Styles

Within each exhibit or program, identify what aspects would satisfy people with the following traits.

How One Thinks—A

(based upon psychological observations)

Left Brain		Right Brain	
Logical		Random	
Sequential		Intuitive	
Rational		Holistic	
Analyze		Synthesize	
Objective		Subjective	
Looks at parts		Looks at whole	

How One Thinks—B

(based upon museum observations)

Describe	
Evaluate	
Classify	
Associate	

How One is "Smart"

(parallels Myers-Briggs personality categories)

What?	How?	Why?	If?
Facts	Problem-solving	Personal connections	Possibilities
Read/listen/ observe/organize	Listen/discuss/ Research/write	Observe/read/ Collect/role-play	Discuss/ imagine/ Design/arrange
Lecture	Inquiry	Share	Non-directive
Closed questions	Open questions	Open questions	Judging questions
Worksheets/ Treasure hunts	Material for Research	Objects for Role-play	Mystery baskets/ art
Identify/locate	Classify/define	Relate to other objects	Pose questions

What Special Skills One Brings

(from Gardner's multiple intelligences)

Verbal-linguistic	
Logical-mathematical	
Visual-spatial	
Body-kinesthetic	
Musical-rhythmic	
Interpersonal	
Intrapersonal	
Naturalistic	

Education Theory Bookshelf

Berk, Laura E., and Adam Winsler. *Scaffolding Children's Learning: Vygotsky and Early Childhood Education*. Washington, D.C.: National Association for the Young Children, 1995.

Csikszentmihalyi, Mihaly. *Flow: The Psychology of Optimal Experience*. New York: Harper Perennial, 1991.

Falk, John H., and Lynn D. Dierking. *Learning from Museums: Visitor Experiences and the Making of Meaning*. Walnut Creek, California: AltaMira Press, 2000.

Gardner, Howard E. *Frames of Mind: The Theory of Multiple Intelligences*. New York: Basic Books, 1983.

—. *Intelligence Reframed: Multiple Intelligences for the 21st Century*. New York: Basics Books, 1999.

Ginsburg, Herbert P., and Sylvia Opper. *Piaget's Theory of Intellectual Development*. Upper Saddle River, New Jersey: Prentice-Hall, Inc., 1987.

Hein, George E., and Mary Alexander. *Museums: Places of Learning*. Washington D.C.: American Association of Museums Education Committee, 1998.

Hildebrand, David. *John Dewey: A Beginner's Guide*. Prescott, Arizona: Oneworld Press, 2008.

Web Bookmarks

About Learning, www.aboutlearning.com.

Group for Education in Museums, www.gem.org.uk/resources/resources_menu.html.

Keller's ARCS Model of Motivational Design, www.arcsmodel.com.

Upclose: The Center for Learning in Out of School Environments, http://upclose.lrdc.pitt.edu/.

Archaeology Education Program
Curriculum Framework

Unit 1	Unit 2	Unit 3
Introduction to Archaeology	Pre-field trip unit	Post-field trip unit
Taught the first 6-7 days of school	Taught one-two weeks prior to scheduled field trips	Taught the week following a class dig/lab
Time span – 6 days	Time span – 5 days	Time span – 3 days
Provides a theme for the fourth grade year, includes basic concepts and skills	Provides a preview of the field trips, includes skills and concepts needed for the three field trips.	Provides follow-up activities that will enable students to process the information
Lessons incorporate hands-on activities, cooperative learning, and problem solving.	Lessons incorporate hands-on and student-centered activities and inquiry-based learning.	Lessons incorporate higher-order thinking skills.
SS/Sci Segment - lessons that deal with terms and concepts used in archaeology that are also specific to fourth grade GPS: such as chronology, sequence of events, observations and inferences, classification, fact and opinion.	SS/Sci Segment – lessons that deal with specific principals and procedures which relate to GPS: mapping and gridding skills, scientific method, characteristics of science, sequence of events, compare and contrast.	SS/Sci Segment – lessons pertaining to the analysis of the students' work. GPS used will include cause and effect, drawing conclusions, scientific method, graphing, chart and table skills, and sequence of events.
ELA Segment – lessons that deal with basic concepts of archaeology and are related to ELA GPS. These lessons will only use one half of the ELA segment. The Research Unit will comprise the rest of the segment.	ELA Segment – Lessons in accordance with GPS using historic fiction, *Phoebe's Secret Diary*, and excerpts from informational sources dealing with the history and actual families from the historic site.	ELA – Revisit the research unit, using results and information to analyze, make conclusions, and write a report. Information and analysis will also be used to interpret the findings and make a display.
Math Segment – 4th grade pacing (No specific lessons included, math integrated in lesson activities.)	Math Segment – 4th grade pacing (No specific lessons included, math integrated in lesson activities.)	Math Segment – 4th grade pacing (No specific lessons included, math integrated in lesson activities.)

- The timeline concept will be introduced in the first unit. Then this will be reinforced throughout the year in the study of social studies. A lesson will be provided with each specific time period to revisit the archaeology theme and allow the students to make a connection between the people and the objects from that time period. This should assist the students with their understanding of the sequence of events in history. Classes will maintain and post time lines in the classroom.
- Since teachers will have introduced the concepts used in archaeology to the class during the first unit, it will be easy to integrate and relate to these concepts throughout the school year, when it is appropriate.

Overview of the Archaeology Education Program

This program is an educational partnership between the Glynn County (Ga.) School System and Fort Frederica National Monument, established to provide a hands-on learning experience for fourth-grade students.

Goal of the Program:

Use archaeology as a method for teaching standards in fourth grade incorporating learning in all curricula areas.

*Use an innovative and hands-on approach to satisfy fourth-grade Georgia Performance Standards.
*Facilitate critical thinking skills, problem solving, and active learning through non-traditional learning activities.
*Provide a creative method of learning about history that reaches the varied learning styles of today's youth.
*Use the scientific method of archaeology to facilitate a multi-disciplinary approach to learn about history.

The Education Program has Four Major Components:

*The curriculum
*A field trip to tour Fort Frederica National Monument
*A pre- and post-dig lesson by the archaeology coordinator
*A two-day field trip for the archaeology field and lab work

Curriculum:

*Lessons designed to give the students appropriate prior knowledge before each of the field trips
*Lessons to provide follow-up activities that will allow the students to expand on the information they have learned from the work at the dig site and in the lab
*Essential questions that are answered by lesson activities in the program involve areas such as:

Discovering how we can learn about history from objects
Using primary sources
Learning about the colonial time period
Use of the scientific method
Mapping and gridding skills
Making observations and inferences
Cause and effect
Drawing conclusions from data
The use of the writing process to write a report based on their experience and conclusions

Fort Field Trip:

*Approximately two and one-half hours in the morning

*Students receive a tour of the town of Frederica, which focuses on showing the characteristics of a colonial town and colonial culture.

*Preparation: reading a historical fiction novel about the colonial time period, mapping exercise about a colonial town, timeline activity, primary source activity about colonial people and their lifestyles.

Pre-Dig Lesson:

*The lesson is scheduled approximately one week prior to a class coming for their field and lab work.

*This lesson is conducted in the participating classroom and involves the use of artifacts and a PowerPoint presentation to show:

*How we learn about history from objects;

*Use of the scientific method in the study of archaeology and history.

*Students will develop several hypotheses about the artifacts they will excavate and what they will learn from the artifacts.

*Two to three pre-dig lessons will be taught at a school on a scheduled day.

Archaeology Dig:

*8:30 until 1:30

*The dig at the Fort Frederica Archaeology Education Site lasts for approximately two and one-half hours.

*Students are transported to the Archaeology Lab at Oglethorpe Point Elementary School to have lunch.

*Students wash the excavated artifacts.

*Students will get to demonstrate the skills they have learned in the classroom.

Archaeology Lab Work:

*8:30 until 1:30 at the school system's Archaeology Lab.

*The lab day will be scheduled the day after the student's fieldwork (dig) day.

*Students will use lab equipment to weigh and measure artifacts, determine how people used the artifacts, and use an analytical process to gather data about their artifacts.

*This data will then be used to help further their understanding of how people lived in the colonial period.

Post-Dig Lesson:

*The lesson is scheduled within the week following a class dig.

*The archaeology coordinator conducts the lesson in the participating group's classroom. The lesson involves processing the data from the lab work to understand what students have learned from the excavated artifacts about colonial life.

*The students will be able to see if the hypotheses that were formed previously in the pre-dig lesson were correct.

*Students will be able to describe and list things that they have learned about this time period of history.

*Students will then be better prepared to write their report on the experience and what they have learned.

*Typically two post-dig lessons are conducted at a school on a scheduled day.

Scheduling:

*Since there are curriculum lessons and activities to be completed prior to the field trips, classes do not start with the field trips until the end of August. There are follow-up lessons to do as well, so the archaeology fieldwork portion ends in mid-May. This will allow those classes digging in May to complete activities, such as the final report, before the school year is over.

*Each school will receive their schedule for their field trips during the first two weeks of school.

Administration of the Program:

*The school system employs an Archaeology Coordinator/Teacher to implement the program in the school system. This is a system-wide employee based at Oglethorpe Point Elementary.

*The coordinator and the Education Park Ranger at Fort Frederica work together to provide a successful program that promotes student learning.

*The Education Park Ranger's primary responsibility is the Fort Frederica field trip, curriculum, and to be the park's representative at the dig site.

*The school system's archaeology coordinator handles all scheduling, curriculum, and the teaching responsibilities for the pre- and post-dig lessons and the field and lab work.

Professional Development Virtual Bookshelf

Association for Supervision and Curriculum Development (www.ASCD.org).

Institute of Museum and Library Services (www.imls.gov)—The Resources section provides many useful IMLS publications related to professional development.

National Association of State Directors of Teacher Education and Certification (www. NASDTEC.org)—This organization chronicles current information related to the continuing education and certification requirements for teachers by state. You must join to look at the Knowledgebase, which is the state-by-state chronicle of incredibly useful information.

National Art Educators Association (www.arteducators.org/olc/pub/NAEA/home/), National Council for the Social Studies (www.socialstudies.org), National Science Teachers Association (www.nsta.org)—These discipline-specific teacher professional organizations are great resources that will lead in other directions.

PBS Teachers (www.pbs.org/teachers/)—The professional development resources provided on this site will give you useful examples of continuing education offerings that meet standards.

Teacher Magazine (www.Teachermagazine.org).

Teacher Sourcebook (www.Teachersourcebook.org).

U.S. Department of Education (http://www.ed.gov)—Look for "Teachers, Professional Development."

Your state's education department—Look for the professional development section.

Websites of museums that offer professional development programs for teachers — Learn from your colleagues. See what they offer and how the programs are developed, structured and evaluated. Call the staff to ask questions. A few to explore: Chicago History Museum (http://www.chicagohs.org/education/educatorprograms), Philadelphia Museum of Art (http://www.philamuseum.org/education/33-232. html), Science Museum of Minnesota (http://www.smm.org/schools/profdev/), Smithsonian American Art Museum (http://americanart.si.edu/education/dev/).

By Discipline

For history and humanities—National Council for History Education (http://www. nche.net/), National Council for Public History (http://ncph.org/cms/), National Endowment for the Humanities (http://www.neh.gov/), National History Day (http://www.nhd.org).

For science—National Science Foundation (http://www.nsf.gov/).

For art—National Endowment for the Arts (http://www.nea.gov/).

Collaboration Bookshelf

Coulson, Ian, and Adrian Norton. *Creating Museum Partnerships with LEA Advisers and Schools.* South East Museum, Library and Archive Council, 2006. <http://www.segfl.org.uk/projects/show/MLA_South_East_-_Creating_museum_partnerships_with_LEA_advisers_and_schools/> .

Dierking, Lynn, John H Falk, Dana Holland, Susan Fisher, Dennis Schatz, and Leila Wilke. *Collaboration: Critical Criteria for Success.* ASTC: Washington, D.C., 1997.

Fox, Louis, and Christine Goodheart. "Creative Schools, Connected Communities: Developing Partnerships for Arts Education." New Horizons for Learning, 2001. <http://www.newhorizons.org/strategies/arts/goodheart2.htm>.

Institute of Museums and Library Services. *True Needs True Partners: Museums Serving Schools*, 1998. <http://imls.gov/pdf/pubtntb.pdf >.

Institute of Museums and Library Services. *Nine to Nineteen: Youth in Museums and Libraries: A Practitioner's Guide.* Washington, D.C., 2008. http://www.imls.gov/news/2008/051608.shtm.

Institute of Museums and Library Services. *Museums, Libraries and 21st Century Skills.* Washington, D.C., 2009. http://www.imls.gov/about/21stCSkills.shtm.

Jusino-Iturralde, Maribel, Claudia Ocello, and Janet Rassweiler. *First Steps: A Scrapbook and Guide for Young Parents, Museums, and Community Partners.* Newark, New Jersey: The New Jersey Historical Society, 2002.

March of Dimes Foundation. *Making Community Partnerships Work: A Toolkit March of Dimes*, 2007. < www.marchofdimes.com/genetics >.

Partnership for 21st Century Skills. *Learning for the 21st Century.* Tucson, Arizona: Partnership for 21st Century Skills, 2002. <http://www.21stcenturyskills.org/index.php>.

Stevenson, Lauren, Elisa Callow, and Emiko Ono. *Interplay: Inspiring Wonder, Discovery, and Learning through Interdisciplinary Museum-Community Partnerships.* Los Angeles: Natural History Museum of Los Angeles County, 2009. http://www.nhm.org/site/sites/default/files/for_teachers/pdf/Full_book_single_01_nhm_interplay_SINGLE.pdf

UMassAmherst, Arts Outreach Extension Service's Learning Partnerships resources - http://www.artsextensionservice.org/index.php/publications/publications-resources/learning-partnerships.

Wagner, Kathleen F., Minda Borun, Jean M. Ferraro, and Julie I. Johnson. *Working Together: Museums and Community Partners.* Philadelphia, PA: PISEC (Philadelphia-Camden Informal Science Education Collaborative), 2000.

LOGIC MODEL – Bakken/MPS Classroom Residency

WHO ☐ hom do we want to impact? ☐ ho will benefit?	VALUES ☐ hat guides our project? ☐ hat do we value in our work?	ASSUMPTIONS ☐ hat do we assume contributes to the effectiveness of our program?	PROCESS How do we expect to bring about the intended changes? ☐ hat are the key activities that will be carried out?	OUTCOMES ☐ hat changes do we hope to bring about as a result of the activities? ☐ hat do we hope to achieve?	IMPACT ☐ hat lasting impact do we hope to have?
Fourth grade students in the Minneapolis Public Schools. Focus is on youth from groups traditionally underrepresented and underserved in science (students of color, students of poverty and girls. A secondary audience is fourth-grade teachers and school-based elementary science specialists.	The Bakken believes that: • Science is a creative process that benefits from diversity. • Society benefits if its citizens are scientifically literate and it scientific workforce represents the diversity of the community. • Scientific advances are most often beneficial to society, improving quality of life and solving local and global problems. • Effective programs for schools are culturally relevant and reflect best practices and standards in K-12 science education. • All young people have the potential and deserve the opportunity to become scientifically-literate citizens and participants in the scientific workforce. • Partnerships are essential to achieving our organizations mission. • Utilization-focused program evaluation guides decision-making and program improvements.	When creative-dramatics instructional strategies are used, more students (especially reluctant learners and those from groups underrepresented and underserved in science) are actively engaged in learning. When students are actively engaged, attitudes improve and more learning occurs. When creative dramatics strategies are used, students can easily connect science to their lives, world and futures. When students possess strong Science Assets*, they will learn and understand science better. When students possess strong Science Assets, they are better prepared to be active citizens and participants in the 21st century workforce.	The Bakken residency is a backward-designed curriculum that: • Uses creative dramatics to engage all students in creative thinking skills especially relevant to science and build their Science Assets*. • Focuses on the following creative thinking skills: – Observing carefully, – Collaborating with others, – Solving problems, – Taking risks and learning from mistakes, and – Using evidence to draw conclusions. • Introduces students to real scientists and engineers and how they use creative thinking skills. • Helps students discover personal relevance for science now and for the future. • Presents science as a human endeavor, blurring interdisciplinary lines and encouraging integration across content areas. • Encourages teachers to use creative-dramatics in their science teaching. • Supports MN Academic Science Standards.	All students will strengthen their Science Assets*, such as: • I know people who value science. I have friends, family, and teachers who use science/science skills in their daily lives. • I can do science. I could be a scientist or engineer. • I use, recognize and value creative thinking skills in science. • Science is relevant to my daily life and to my future. It is important to the world around me. • Science is often used for social good. Differences in Science Assets* based on gender or ethnicity will be reduced. Students will become more engaged in science in school. Students will become more effective science learners and demonstrate their knowledge and understanding.	Students (especially students of color, students of poverty and girls) hold attitudes, beliefs, knowledge and skills that are indicators for success in science. Differences in science attitudes, beliefs, knowledge and skills based on gender, ethnicity/race, and socioeconomic status are reduced. All students (especially students of color, students of poverty and girls) are prepared to be scientifically-literate citizens who recognize scientific issues, think creatively and solve problems. Student achievement in science is increased and the science achievement gap is reduced. High-quality science instruction influences student achievement and reduces the achievement gap in other disciplines.

*Science Assets are a set of strength-based attitudes, based on research and experience, that indicate students' perseverance in science and prepare students for life after school in terms of civic engagement and job opportunities.

Acknowledgement: This form and instruction on its use was provided by Mary Ellen S. Murphy, Evaluation and Planning Consultant, Minneapolis, MN.

Paying-For-It Bookshelf

Dropkin, Murray, and Bill La Touche. *The Budget-Building Book for Nonprofits: A Step-by-Step Guide for Managers and Boards.* 2nd ed. San Francisco, California: Jossey-Bass Publishers, 2007.

This practical "how to" book provides basic information and budget templates but must be adapted to accommodate education projects and programs.

Keating, Elizabeth K. "Is There Enough Overhead in This Grant?" *Nonprofit Quarterly* 10 (Spring 2003): 41–44.

Understanding the true cost of a project's overhead can significantly impact its success. This article provides information as to how to calculate these costs in order to determine whether the program will benefit the organization or will require more work than the program is worth.

Kotler, Neil, Philip Kotler, and Wendy Kotler. *Museum Marketing and Strategy: Designing Missions, Building Audiences, Generating Revenue and Resources.* 2nd ed. San Francisco, California: John Wiley & Sons, 2008.

This book aids in understanding how to successfully communicate program information in a competitive marketplace and develop a consumer-centered museum.

Olenick, Arnold J., Philip R. Olenick, Foundation Center. *A Nonprofit Organization Operating Manual: Planning for Survival and Growth.* New York: Foundation Center, 1991.

This manual provides detailed information about the many practical aspects of managing non- profit finances. Although not specific to educational programming, understanding finances in the context of the larger organization is important to a program or department's overall success.

The Museum Learning Process™

NYCMS students work in museum galleries a minimum of two afternoons a week. The collections represent traditions of intellectual rigor and high standards that provide the basis for interdisciplinary learning. Faced with scientific specimens, works of art, historical documents, and artifacts, students learn to construct their own knowledge. By attending the museum regularly, students become skilled at the museum learning process—extended observation, questioning, research, synthesis and analysis, presentation, and reflection—that is based on the process of discovery exemplified by the work of museum professionals.

NYCMS students are taught different strategies—taking notes, comparing and contrasting, sketching, and describing in oral and written formats—to improve their **extended observation** skills. They look closely at primary sources, extract information from the exhibited items, and look at the context in which these items are displayed.

NYCMS students engage in models of scholarship found in museums that complement work done in the classroom. They participate in the museum learning process by **asking questions** about the objects and discerning which questions can be answered by further observation and which require additional **research**.

Students learn to utilize a range of resources including textbooks, literature, the Internet, other museums and collections, and subject specialists in the museums and at school to gather information. Students develop the skills necessary to **synthesize and analyze** information from different sources, and to make decisions about how to use the information.

Students experience a variety of high quality **presentation** models in the galleries, publications, and programs of our partner museums. Over the course of their experience at NYCMS, students are expected to move toward these professional presentation standards in their own work through an on-going assessment and **reflection** process.

Although NYCMS students are introduced to the museum learning process in the galleries and halls of our partner museums, they utilize the process in their school-based subject classes when confronting a mathematical problem, designing a scientific experiment, studying a new map, or reading difficult text.

The Museum Learning Process and Math

(Based on the 9th grade POW-Style Write-Up sheet developed by Faith Muirhead)

Extended Observation
(5 points)—After reading or listening to the problem, you must restate in writing what you are being asked to do. You should be clear and precise. Use math vocabulary if you can.

Questioning
(3 points)—What questions did you ask yourself? Which questions did you decide to answer? Why?

Research
(5 points)—Tell me what you did to gather data for your explanation.
    How did you get started?
    What approaches did you try?
    What information did you gather?
    When did you decide to stop and why?
    How did you check your answer?

Analysis and Synthesis
(5 points)—What did you find as possible answers to the questions? What rules or patterns did you discover? Explain why you think a particular rule works.

Reflection
(5 points)—Reflection should happen in many stages of solving the problem. You need to reflect on your work if you come to a dead end or your answer does not check. What did you find difficult about this problem? If it was easy, how could you change it to make it more challenging?

Presentation
(2 points)—Make sure that all of the parts of your work are labeled, that the work is neat, and that you have used full sentences in your explanations.

Object Observation

Educators at the Brooklyn Museum of Art originally developed the Object Observation exercise as a strategy for honing their skills as careful lookers and gallery teachers. NYC Museum School teachers have refined it for use with students, and in the words of a NYCMS high school history teacher:

> While this process is designed to facilitate teaching and learning in the museum, I find it equally applicable to the traditional academic classroom. It is useful to be able to ask students to study a piece of text, a map, a political cartoon or a graph with the same care and attention to detail with which they study a painting or an object of art. —Jill Bloomberg, U.S. History teacher

Throughout their classes, New York City Museum School (NYCMS) students engage in The Museum Learning Process™. Students do extended observations; engage in questioning; employ research skills to study from a variety of sources; analyze and synthesize information; present their findings in many formats; and reflect on their learning process and work, through peer and professional critiques. Each of these steps is closely aligned with the literacy work being done in our school district.

During the extended observation and questioning processes students are engaged in "accountable talk." They must observe the object, document, or exhibit closely, describe it objectively and subjectively, and formulate questions. "What do you see that made you ask that question?" "Where do you see that?" As students master this process, teachers become less and less involved. The students hold each other accountable for their observations.

In the museum galleries, Object Observation is designed to:

1. encourage longer and closer looking skills;

2. increase articulation skills, by focusing on the use of descriptive language;

3. develop interpretation skills, or the ability to discern and extrapolate information based on observation and previous knowledge vs. that which requires new research;

4. stimulate curiosity, and the quest for additional information;

5. emphasize the possibilities of new research; and, begin a process of synthesizing information (from observation, research, questioning, listening to and conferring with colleagues) that ultimately leads to new understanding.

In addition, Object Observation encourages educators to:

*use listening as a teaching and learning tool, and;
*incorporate diverse perspectives, interests, concerns and skills.

Object Observation Exercise

1. Observation and Recording

>After selecting an object, divide a piece of paper into two columns. (See the attached sheet.) Without any introduction to the object, or (if in a museum) without reading the label, take 10 -15 minutes to record observations that are:
>
>a.   OBJECTIVE (Describe what can be perceived by the senses, e.g., sight or touch. Students begin to understand that they can describe color, size, shape, texture, and parts of the whole or specific details. It is difficult to find the language that will describe something objectively.)
>
>b.   SUBJECTIVE (What does this object make you think about? What does it remind you of? Students understand that prior knowledge, cultural biases, stories, and their own imagination give them insights into what they experience.)
>
>List 3–5 questions about the object.
>
>You may also want to make a sketch of the object, noting colors, etc.

2. Sharing Observations

Individuals present their objective and subjective observations and their questions to others in the group.

3. Presentation of Available Information and Research

When available, the group leader presents label information, curatorial notes from catalogue entries, related myths, stories, etc.

4. Discussion

The group compares their observations and insights with the information presented, and notes which questions were answered and which questions require further research.

Object Observation

OBJECTIVE Describe the object.	SUBJECTIVE What does it make you feel/think about?

QUESTIONS
What do you wonder? What do you want to know?

_____

_____

_____

_____

_____

_____

About the Authors

Betsy Bowers strives to bring positive meaningful museum experiences to diverse audiences. During many years as a Qm2 consultant, she worked with multiple museums including the Smithsonian, Roanoke Island Festival Park and the National Building Museum. Currently, she is Director of Education and Visitor Experience for the National Law Enforcement Museum, due to open in Washington, DC, in 2013. She is a graduate and past adjunct faculty member of The George Washington University Museum Education Program.

James Boyer, Ph.D., is the Director of Children's Education at The New York Botanical Garden, where he oversees all student and teacher programs. Before becoming the director, he taught and managed the Garden's Professional Development Program for Teachers including the Urban Advantage Program. He holds a doctorate in Botany from the State University of New York, and has over 15 years of experience teaching informal, science-based education to all ages.

Ronald Chaluisan, founding co-principal of The New York City Museum School, is currently Vice President for Programs at New Visions for Public Schools, the largest education reform organization in NYC. Previously he led the New Century High Schools Initiative, a comprehensive school creation process, and designed supports for existing small schools. Mr. Chaluisan holds a B.A. from Harvard University, an M.A. from Claremont Graduate University and an M.Ed. from Bank Street College of Education.

Ann Fortescue, Director of Education and Visitor Services at the Senator John Heinz History Center, joined the staff in 1990 and has participated in nearly every aspect of the Center's development. Ann completed the Getty's Museum Leadership Institute in 2009. She holds an M.S. in museum education from Bank Street College of Education in New York City and a B.A. in history from Bates College in Maine.

Kim Fortney is Deputy Director of National History Day in College Park, Maryland. Previously she explored history education through the lens of the museum, devoting 13 years to the field as Education Curator, then Vice President of the Heritage Center of Lancaster County in Lancaster, Pa. Kim earned an M.A. in History and Museum Studies from Duquesne University and a B.A. in History and Secondary Education from Westminster College. She is a certified teacher in Pennsylvania.

Amy Goicoechea (contributor) is the Associate Curator of Education at the National Museum of Wildlife Art in Jackson Hole, Wyoming. She cherishes the opportunity to teach in gorgeous galleries surrounded by fine art. Amy has worked as an educator her entire professional career. She began as a philosophy instructor, became a religion teacher, and now enjoys being an educator in a unique setting that affords varied and rich interpretive and instructional possibilities.

Beth Twiss Houting, the Director of Education for the Chester County Historical Society in Pennsylvania, has worked in and consulted for a variety of museums over the last 30 years, including

Winterthur and the National Constitution Center. Her special areas of interest are hands-on object learning, exhibition interactivity, and visitor research. Beth has an MA in the Winterthur Program in Early American Culture with a Museum Studies certificate from the University of Delaware.

Julie I. Johnson, the Science Museum of Minnesota's John Roe Distinguished Chair of Museum Leadership, provides strategic leadership in planning, programming, personnel development and collaboration. She has served as Program Officer for National Science Foundation and faculty for the Getty Leadership Institute. As VP of Education and COO for the New Jersey State Aquarium, she spearheaded community and youth programs and PISEC's "Family Science Learning Study and Families Exploring Science Together." Currently she serves on the board of the Visitor Studies Association.

Maria Marable-Bunch has created and implemented numerous professional development programs for Pre-K–12 teachers on how to use museum objects to enhance classroom instruction and improve student learning. She has an extensive background in working with superintendents, curriculum specialists, principals, teachers, parents, and other educational specialists in creating in-depth programs and educational resources, in print and on the web, that draw on museum resources.

Elizabeth (Beth) Murphy is the Director of Special Projects at The Bakken Museum in Minneapolis, where she directs the School Partnership Program and is especially involved in teacher professional development and program evaluation. She is considered a "hidden physicist," having left a more traditional career path 10 years ago to join the informal science education community. She also serves on the executive committee of SciMathMN, a statewide coalition advocating for quality K–12 STEM education.

Claudia Ocello, President & CEO, Museum Partners Consulting, LLC, winner of multiple national museum awards, has over 20 years experience in museums with education programs, exhibitions, accessibility issues, and evaluation projects. At The NJ Historical Society she planned and worked with museum-school partnerships. Claudia co-teaches in the Masters in Museum Professions Program at Seton Hall University. She earned an M.S. in Museum Education from Bank Street College of Education and previously taught 5th grade.

Mark D. Osterman has been working in the educational field for the past 11 years, focusing on arts-integrated curriculum and museum-school collaborations. He has worked for the Miami-Dade County Public Schools, The Wolfsonian–FIU, Brooklyn Museum Art, and Museum of Arts and Design. He has a BFA from the School of Visual Arts, an MA from New York University, and is currently obtaining a doctorate from Florida International University.

Ellen Provenzano (contributor) has a BS in Secondary Education, an MS in Post Secondary Education, and has taught students in grades four through 12. Since 1995 she has been the Archaeology Education Coordinator for the Glynn County Georgia school system. As the administrator for an award-winning program for fourth graders, she is responsible for program implementation, curriculum development, training teachers, and the coordination and instruction of fourth grade classes during their participation in the archaeology program.

Janet Rassweiler is Acting Director and faculty advisor for the Leadership in Museum Education graduate program at Bank Street College of Education. She also heads her own consulting practice, which furthers arts, culture, and community collaborations. Her 20+ years of experience in the field includes leadership positions at Young Audiences New York and at The New Jersey

Historical Society, where she was instrumental in transforming the institution from an exclusive to inclusive community-based organization.

Kathrine Walker Schlageck, Senior Educator, Marianna Kistler Beach Museum of Art, has 25 years of art and history museum education experience, including creating her current program. She specializes in developing art-integrated programs for schools and has published four curricula. She mentors and teaches education students at Kansas State University and presents professionally. She received two awards from the NAEA, a service award from MPMA EdCom, and the 2009 Kansas Governor's Award for Art Education.

Beverly Sheppard is the President of the Institute for Learning Innovation, a center for learning research and evaluation in museums. Her museum experience spans 25 years and includes positions as Acting Director of the Institute of Museum and Library Services and as CEO of Old Sturbridge Village in Massachusetts. Beverly is co-author of *Thriving in a Knowledge Age: New Business Models for Museums and Other Cultural Institutions,* with John H. Falk, and editor of *Building Museum and School Partnerships*, a predecessor to this book.

Marla Shoemaker is The Kathleen C. Sherrerd Senior Curator of Education at the Philadelphia Museum of Art, responsible for the activities of a large and diverse department whose programs serve some 200,000 museum visitors annually. She has authored and edited articles on museum teaching as well as numerous gallery guides for parents and children, most recently co-authoring a children's picture book, *A is for Art Museum,* and the teaching resource, *Art Speaks.*

James Stein, a museum educator at the Philadelphia Museum of Art, is Coordinator of Art Speaks. He has co-presented sessions on Art Speaks at local and national conferences and was previously a museum educator at the National Gallery of Art, Washington, DC. He holds a B.A. from Yale University, a J.D. from Villanova University School of Law, and an M. S. Ed. in Leadership in Museum Education from the Bank Street College of Education.

Ellen Strojan (contributor) has been employed by the National Park Service for over 16 years. She currently works at Fort Frederica National Monument on Saint Simons Island, Ga., with the historical archaeology education partnership program and manages the park bookstore. In 1990 she graduated with a B.A. degree in Speech Communications from Edinboro University of Pennsylvania. In 2002 she earned an M.A. in Teaching/Museum Education from The George Washington University.

Keni Sturgeon is Mission Mill Museum's Curator, as well as adjunct faculty at Western Oregon University, Linfield College and the University of Oklahoma, teaching Museum Studies courses. Previously she was the Curator for Programs and Education at Brown University's Haffenreffer Museum of Anthropology. She received her M.A. in Anthropology and Museum Studies from Arizona State University. She is the Chair of AAM's Committee on Audience Research and Evaluation, and Secretary of the Oregon Museums Association.

Jennifer Michaelree Squire began her museum "career" at age nine and is a strong believer in the power of museums and making personal connections. Currently she is the Education Director of Dumbarton House, and has worked or volunteered at the National Building Museum, Discovery Creek Children's Museum of Washington, The International Spy Museum, Play With Words Children's Museum, and The Cold War Museum. She is a graduate of The George Washington University Museum Education Program.

Sonnet Takahisa, founding co-director of The New York City Museum School, is currently Director of Education at the National 9/11 Memorial & Museum, where she is developing teaching and learning activities. She worked at the Boston Children's Museum, Seattle Art Museum, and Brooklyn Museum and consults on museums, arts education, public engagement and educational reform. She coordinates the Museum-School Partnership Learning Network, a NY group focused on improving student success.

Mary Jane Taylor is Program Developer at the National Constitution Center in Philadelphia. She has 16 years of experience in exhibition interpretation, interactive and audio tour development and visitor research. She also has extensive background in creating, administering and evaluating tours and programs for teacher, school and family audiences. She has degrees from the Winterthur Program in Early American Culture at the University of Delaware, James Cook University of North Queensland and Wittenberg University.

Laura Dickstein Thompson has 20 years of experience in art/museum education. As Director of Exhibitions and Education for Kidspace at MASS MoCA, Thompson has brought about Kidspace's expanded gallery, developed award-winning programs and resources, and curated highly-acclaimed Kidspace exhibitions with world renowned artists. Thompson also serves as a museum consultant, and is an assistant professor of art history at the Massachusetts College of Liberal Arts. She holds a doctorate from Columbia University Teachers College.

Courtney Waring (contributor) is Director of Education at the Delaware Art Museum. Since 2006 she has acted as Program Coordinator for Project ART SCOPE (Students Creating, Observing, Participating and Engaging), a unique multiple-visit program in collaboration with the Christina Cultural Arts Center and Kuumba Academy Charter School. She holds a B.A. and M.A. in Art History, in addition to a graduate-level teacher's certification in Elementary Education from West Chester University.

Julia Washburn is a conservation-education professional with more than 20 years of experience working to help people of all ages form deep personal connections with their environment and heritage. She provides education planning and program design services for museums, non-profit organizations, parks, and conservation agencies through her consulting business, Trillium Resources Group. She also teaches in the Museum Education Program at George Washington University Graduate School.

Susy Watts, a board member of EdCom for eight years, consults on strategic planning, evaluation and teaching and learning for museums and schools. Projects include LACMA On-site education programs; Washington Arts Education Resources Initiative II; Honolulu Academy of Arts, strategic planning; Idaho State Historical Society, strategic planning; Portland Japanese Gardens, teacher training; and Center for Wooden Boats at-risk youth programs. She serves as teaching and learning consultant for four U.S. Department of Education AEMDD and PDAE grants.

Jean Woodley, Project Advisor, serves as liaison between Art Speaks and the School District of Philadelphia. A former art teacher and an experienced museum educator, she has worked extensively with school students, parents, teachers and administrators. In addition to developing educational programming and teaching materials for the classroom, she has served as consultant to museum volunteers and professional staffs alike, especially those with the goal of fostering inclusiveness and audience diversity.

Index

AMERICAN ASSOCIATION OF MUSEUMS

Your Resource, Voice, Community

Be a part of the largest museum association—the national service organization that represents your professional interests. Membership brings you exceptional benefits:

- Expert help and confidential, customized guidance on any museum matter, from finance and ethics to facilities management and collection stewardship—*AAM's Information Center*

- Deep discounts on education and professional development opportunities—*AAM's Annual Meeting and MuseumExpo™*, *Seminars* and *Webinars*

- Access to the most complete, accurate and timely information for and about museums —*Museum* magazine, *Aviso Online* and *AAM Action Alerts & Legislative Updates*

- Significant discounts on professional literature covering every museum subject from audience research to technology —the *AAM Bookstore*

- Opportunities to network with colleagues who work in the same field or have similar interests —*AAM's Standing Professional Committees* and *Professional Interest Committees*

- A voice in Washington to make the case for museums with Congress, policymakers and the media —*AAM's Government Relations Department* and *Museum Advocacy Day*

- Collective buying power of more than 20,000 members to save you time and money on insurance, shipping and other services—*AAM's Affinity Partner Program*

- Opportunities to apply for funding assistance for AAM professional development—*AAM Fellowships*

- Ability to receive instant alerts about new job opportunities and post your resume so that hundreds of museums can find you—*AAM's JobHQ*

"The wheels are in motion to use the webinar series as a professional development opportunity for many of our staff. We thank you for modeling this way of learning and for making great information and people available to us at such reasonable prices. **It is yet another way my AAM membership gives me value!"** —*Connie Bodner, Ohio Historical Society, Columbus OH*

Join AAM Today

For more information on becoming a member and all the member benefits and discounts visit
www.aam-us.org/joinus or call **866.226.2150.**